Radiant Relationships

Holistic Coaches Share How
Radiant Your Relationships Can Be

Co-Authored by Holistic Coaches
Trained by Radiant Coaches Academy

RadiantCoaches.com

RADIANT RELATIONSHIPS

RADIANT RELATIONSHIPS

Copyright © 2018 Radiant Publishing

All rights reserved.

CONTENTS

"Love Attracts Love" by Dez Stephens – page 1

"It Starts and Ends with You" by Dr. Thurman E. Webb – page 7

"Free to be ME" by Karen Kipke – page 19

"My New Form of Church" by Charneva McKeller – page 25

"Be Your Own Hero" by Krystalyn Norton – page 38

"Radiance is Created" by Nichole Terry – page 45

"Radiant Relationship with Myself" by Kiki Dombrowski – page 60

"The Stormwall" by Jessie Jean Damico – page 80

"Radiant Fairy Tales" by Shenetta Matthews – page 107

"Radiant Trust" by Tamala Davis – page 116

"Mirror Mirror on the Wall" by Amanda North – page 128

"Social Media Social" by Lindsey Rhodes – page 139

"Human Connection" by Sara Smith – page 149

"How Can I Make My Relationships Not Suck?" by Mai White – page 161

"Dee, Momma is Dead" by Adia Moreno – page 179

Radiant Coaches Academy *(a division of Radiant Health Institute)* is a social enterprise and prominent coach training school that certifies holistic life coaches, wellness coaches and business coaches.

RADIANT RELATIONSHIPS

Love Attracts Love

by Dez Stephens

I have always had an incredible ability to love. As a child, I was somehow able to instantaneously forgive people as they were harming me. As an adult, I have become a fierce love warrior.

As a life coach, I am constantly asked about finding love. In my opinion, the quickest way to find love is to love yourself. But how?

The answer to that question is unique for every individual. Ask yourself how this can best be done. Is it letting something go? Is it speaking kindly to yourself? Maybe it's just realizing that you are worthy of love.

Having a healthy relationship with yourself is critical. It doesn't matter a flip-dip whether someone else likes or loves you. What matters is can you receive it well. What matters more is how you see the other person as a reflection of your own love.

For example, falling in love with someone is a form of falling in love with yourself. The "other" is a mirror – a reflection of your own self. Their beauty is your own.

An elderly couple interviewed about their longterm marriage was asked, "What do you see when you look at your spouse?" The wife responded, "I see me" with a huge smile on her face.

Another question to ask yourself is, "How much do I love myself?" Sometimes it's not about people not loving themselves – it's a matter of how they might not fully love themselves.

Having a radiant relationship with yourself is a great beginning to drawing in love from others. It's the "like attracts like" principle – love simply attracts more love.

Have you ever noticed how loving people are surrounded by other loving people? Have you noticed the ones who are negative about love are surrounded by others who are also negative about love and relationships? Look around and notice who's there.

Notice what you're noticing. Feel what you're feeling. Observe your thoughts and feelings about relationships.

Are you open? Are you optimistic? Are you hanging onto old stories that are holding you back from healthy relationships?

Ask yourself how radiant you want your relationships to be. Some of us don't want the shiny-happy-people experience. Some of us do.

Do you want to be generous in your relationships? Are you ready to be the recipient of generosity from others?

We are always being matched. We are paired up with those who are like us – similar to our energy. This is true for our co-workers, friends, family members, lovers, companions and others.

If you want a new relationship to show up, ask yourself who you want to arrive. Then clearly envision this person. Picture them right in front of you. Then ask yourself if you're ready for this person and this new relationship.

This kind of self-examination is a great way to gauge where you're at in terms of the kinds of people you need and want in your life. It's also a good way to measure your interest in new relationships.

Either way, we are in relationships. The decision we face daily is whether we want these relationships to be healthy, whole and radiant (or not).

If we want healthy, we need to be healthy. If we want whole, we need to be whole. If we want radiant, we need to embody radiance.

Being a healthy person is about caring deeply for yourself – taking good care of yourself. Being a whole person is about having a holistic approach to living – not neglecting any part of your life. Being a radiant person is about exuding love at its highly level – loving yourself fully.

"I am love" is a great affirmation to use daily. Your subconscious responds best when you repeat this affirmation first thing in the morning as you're waking.

The second you realize you're awake. Say it in your head. Say it aloud. Say it in and out of meditation or prayer. Speak it often. You will feel a difference in your life almost immediately.

The bottom line is that love is easy to attract. Radiant relationships are easy to obtain. Having a loving mindset brings more love in your life.

So ask yourself how ready you are for all these new radiant relationships!

RADIANT RELATIONSHIPS

It Starts and Ends with You

by Dr. Thurman E. Webb

Over the years, working in the counseling profession, I have encountered various individuals who have defined their relationship situation as nonproductive and stymied. These people often want advice on how to improve their relationships, how to form more meaningful and productive relationships, and/or how to exit dysfunctional relationships.

Before we move any further, let's be clear on one thing. If the person you are seeking advice from starts the conversation with, "If I was you" or, "If I was in that situation," understand you are about to receive some deficient and in most cases BAD advice.

They are emphatically not YOU, and they are definitely not YOU in that situation. Understanding that, let's continue. Renovating and creating healthy productive relationships starts and ends with YOU.

YOU ultimately decide what you want in your life and what its role will be for life. Relationships aren't just about bonds and connections between people, they are also about interactions between situation, places, and the SELF, yes the SELF.

When I mention having a relationship with the SELF people often look at me side-eyed. But let's look at it, how often do you engage in conversations with yourself? How often do you consult yourself in a moment? How often do you talk or persuade yourself to act differently than you feel? In my opinion, the SELF is the fountainhead for all radiant relationships.

When we look at stagnate relationships we have to look for commonalities. By analyzing your current relationships and identifying the common themes that sustain their existence you can identify key pieces to your relational puzzles. Ironically, the key difference between progress and stagnation is the same key difference between excuses and explanations - - PERSONAL RESPONSIBILITY!!

Personal responsibility allows you to see things clearly and recognize those things you can and cannot control. This clarity results in an increased probability that you will have a more meaningful impact on your desired relational target.

I'm sure, like me, you are no stranger to hearing the phrase, "I just seem to have bad luck with Men and/or women" and "It seems like bad situations just find me." Statements like these are the breeding grounds for excuses that lead to stagnation.

Statements like these support the idea of external locus of control. Statements like these do not lead to an empowering revelation about relationship building. Relationship building is a continuous process of give and take, and when done correctly never feels daunting. You are the gatekeeper to all things YOU. What does that mean?

It means that you have the power and control to decide who, what, and why something is a part of your life. Knowing who you are and embracing your identity allows you to set the guidelines and boundaries by which others will interact with you.

You decide what is acceptable and what is not. You decide if you stay, how long you stay, and when you leave. When people are able to come to this realization, more often than not, they are able to approach relationship building in a more organic way.

It prevents them from becoming subservient to "chance" outcomes and allows them to take an active stance in maintaining their relationship building construct. This active stance nurtures your confidence, which in turn results in increased control over relationship outcomes.

Organic relationship building involves creating a space that accounts for your cognitive and instinctual prowess, then accepting and trusting the resolution that comes out of the collaboration between the two.

The relationships you form with your identity and purpose contributes immensely to your individual relationship building construct. That's not to say that the relationships you have with people and organizations aren't important, because they are. They are the means by which you control your external stimuli.

However, how you translate the information that comes out of interpersonal interaction is determined by the understanding you have about yourself, situations, and yourself in situations.

Building a viable relationship between the person you are, the person you want to be, and the person you should be allows you to monitor your development while in the transition.

Building a healthy relationship with YOU will aid you in figuring out who or what you are passionate about, and that will give you some sort of roadmap to guide you toward what is purposeful and/or what your purpose is.

Forming a healthy and unapologetic identity through truthful, satisfying, and purposeful introspection provides you the luxury to require others do the same if they want to be a part of your life.

Through various forms of research it has been proven that human beings naturally want to commune and belong, and we experience various forms of happiness from these interactions.

That's not to say that one cannot find happiness in the company of oneself. It means that our interpersonal and intrapersonal aptitude work together to create plans for productive relationship building.

Relationships are comprised of two or more individuals interacting and influencing each other in various ways. Understating the aforementioned, what are the criteria for the relationships you build?

Generally we form relationships with people and situations that make us feel good and provide us with good benefits. These benefits don't always have to be equal, however, many people who deem themselves in a healthy relationship or situation require it to be equitable.

One of the concerns with weighing your relationships on the benefit scale is that it opens the door for the, "What have you done for me lately" ideology. In these types of relationships it is not uncommon for individuals to form an allegiance to the benefit and not the person, so when the benefit is gone so is the person.

In 1969 John Bowlby wrote a book titled Attachment, and in it he explained how secure attachments, specifically those to your mother and father, aid us in dealing with stresses later in life.

His writings lend themselves to the idea that adults who have a healthy attachment style are more likely to build relationships that are satisfying and purposeful. We naturally evaluate (not define) who we are by observing other people, situations, and people in situations around us.

The results from our contemplative evaluations play a critical role in how we form our relationships because they often lead to questions about who we, or reaffirm who we know we are.

Do you build relationships that are continuous? Do you build relationships that are exclusive or inclusive? These, and questions like these, are integral to relationship building that is productive and fulfilling.

I am well aware that when most people talk about relationships they talk about them in terms of person to person interaction. But in a world where the sun affects the land and the moon affects the ocean; where animals have a keen sense for the weather and all it encompasses; where smells can trigger specific memories; and where songs can evoke various emotions, it is only fitting that the definition of relationships be expanded to include everything around YOU.

Relationships are a byproduct of how we relate. How we relate is based on how we send and receive information. The information flow is regulated by our acceptance of people and situations around us.

Acceptance is a vital piece to healthy and functional relationships. Acceptance is at the core of appreciating life as a whole. Paradoxically, you don't have to understand why some things happen or why people are the way they are to accept them. Acceptance is your willingness to believe in and/or come to terms with a given thing or situation.

Accepting people, things, and situation for what they are gives you the power and clarity to influence and change the situation or change YOU in the situation. Acceptance allows you to open your mind to realistic and truthful outcomes. The journey to quality relationship building can be made easier through accepting what it takes to get there.

Most people want relationships that are fulfilling; however, they under sale themselves and settle for a "caring" that is comfortable and convenient rather than a "love" that is complimenting and considerate. Next time you're looking to establish a fulfilling relationship try and find a connection through a love of happiness.

As you develop an authentic sense of SELF, people will appreciate their relationship with YOU, and you will start to establish healthy and fulfilling relationships with everything around you. Some people may ask "what should you expect to gain from your relationships?"

Here's a thought, expect to understand yourself better today than you did yesterday. Expect to define and build your relationships with others with a clear understanding of yourself. Relationships are a construct that allows you to see yourself through the lens of communal togetherness bonded by a love and appreciation for being YOU.

As you work toward improving your scholarship in relationship building remember that all of your senses play a role in the process, and accepting the information you get from your senses is vital. Like everything we do, building a relationship is a process.

Working on your process for building healthy relationships is what ultimately affects the type of relationship you form. Your actions are a decision, and all actions have an intention.

RADIANT RELATIONSHIPS

Free to be ME

by Karen Kipke

"Dream Big" as the famous quote goes. And so we dream. We dream of the far off vacations in exotic lands. We dream of Mr. Right or Ms. Right, the extreme perfect being to satisfy all our needs. We dream of the luxury in the form of yachts, expensive cars and mansions.

We dream of drinking from the fountain of youth, to look and feel younger for one more day. We dream of the endless happiness overflowing our cup. Yet no one I have ever met tells me they dream of loving themselves completely.

We search, we seek, we ponder, we stress, we settle, we drain our bank accounts looking for the answer to the almighty question: What is the key to happiness? All you have to do is look in the mirror. You are the key to your ultimate happiness. You were born with all the tools you need to create happiness in your life. Stop being so harsh on yourself and your shortcomings. Make a resolution to only pay yourself compliments and focus on your strengths.

Wow! What would that feel like, seeking the answer from within instead of constantly trying to find the answers externally? We trick ourselves into believing that others know better than we do. Truly listen to your inner voice, the one that loves you and wishes the best for you, the inner voice that will guide you to your fullest version of yourself. Feel empowered to break down the barriers and allow yourself to become whoever you wish to be.

Upon reading an interview with Matthew McConaughey after he won the Oscar for Best Actor 2014, his quote captured me, "I was forced to get to know myself better because I was stuck with nobody but me and me only." This quote reminded me of my younger self as I tried to find my place in the world in my early 20's and then some in my 30's.

As I enter my 40's, life teaches me to live my life on

my terms. When I am my greatest expression of myself, I am able to fully love myself. I find I have more love to offer the world and in return others love me more powerfully too.

Life delivers this terrible yo-yo effect of being who you wish to be and being what others think you should be. Whose opinion matters most, the other person's opinion of you or your opinion of yourself? We, as humans, seek approval, and so we place false importance on what other's think is right for us in our lives. Unfortunately, we fall into this trap where we long to be someone else.

Often times we hear people comment, "I wish I could be more like her" or "He's got it all". We place such a distorted sense of perfection on other people. By all means, admire and respect the person for that specific quality you feel they possess. Are they better than you? Certainly not! More qualified to be you? Absolutely not!

"Follow your passion," people say. Then they spend all day advising you on how to follow your passion correctly and even go as far as to tell you that you are doing it wrong! Yikes! What I like most about the thousands of young people auditioning for *American Idol* is that no matter if they sing well or like a dying cat, they stand tall in front of the judges with confidence and an unwavering belief in themselves.

No, everyone should not get the golden ticket to Hollywood, but everyone should have that shining moment of belief in their abilities, passion in their cause, and faith in their dream. What was your last shining star moment?

Allow yourself to love you for your hard work, your talents, your compassion and your wisdom. Have the courage to take a stand and love yourself completely with flaws and all. Enjoy where you are in your life. Enjoy whatever you are going through; all your tangled messes, your indecision, finding your way through life's labyrinth.

Take charge of your life. When you do what is right for you, you glow and it's contagious. People want to feel that glow. They believe in your power. They start to look up to you as a leader.

Yes, Dream Big! Dream to be free in your own skin. Reclaim your life: I am me, I am free, I am Free to be Me!

RADIANT RELATIONSHIPS

My New Form of Church
by Charneva McKeller

Going to church was never a bad experience for me. It wasn't just awesomely radiant, but it wasn't a bad experience. As a child I remember the food that was often served at the various anniversaries and celebrations. I remember the Mother Board and those cute little ladies and their big pretty hats.

The preacher who was male or female has always been the best-dressed, shiniest, most confident person in the building. As I grew into an adolescent I remember lock-ins where we would just stay at the church overnight. The boys from the age of 12 up to 16 years were always there. I do believe they were the only reason I was there. There were so many cute boys.

This is simply what went on in my first encounters with what was supposed to be my path and connection with the Divine. As I got older and started making new choices, I was still force-fed helpings of the same meal. There was no spiritual radiance and no effulgence… But I went to church because that is the only way I knew how to create and build that personal relationship with my Divine. This was the only way I was shown, the only way in my family that was known.

I have always been one of those "there is something greater" dreamers. However, in my life I have settled for a few things. I started to believe there were no more Unicorns. I accepted that Prince Charming had a lot of things going on that were not shown in any Disney Princess movie that, had I known, would have made me think twice about getting married so young. I also thought that not everyone had good intentions.

One thing that I refuse up to this day is to settle for a mundane relationship with my Divine. I have cried at church, the choirs always get me when they are good. But I can watch The Voice tv show and get teary eyed as well. I love music; good music touches my spirit no matter where I hear it.

I have been emotional a few times at church. But they weren't those "something greater" emotions. There is nothing greater than God. That is definitely not what I meant. I mean something greater for me, something that I could feel; the way that the lady who was running around the church felt.

I wanted to pass out like everyone else who felt the Spirit. I wanted to shine like they were shining. I wanted a strong Divine relationship. After a while, since I didn't feel the connection, I completely stopped going to church. There was no radiance for me there. I felt empty! I felt that I needed to find out more about spirituality not religion. Different stories fascinated me.

To this day I love a good myth. I am becoming more and more a modern day mystic, surrendering to the truth. I am intrigued by the comparison of spiritual text from different religion. So I already know the base story line. I needed to find a path, one that created that connection with my Divine and me. I knew ours wasn't the story that I was force-fed all my life; ours was something different and magical. Ours was that something greater.

For a while there was no Divine interaction. I didn't know where to start to get where I needed.

So I went nowhere. I always have my family in my ear telling me my life would be better if I were to go back church. I was not against church. I've just never believed it was an essential meeting point for me and my Divine. So going back to church wouldn't have made a difference, I would've just been there.

A marriage and two babies took up most of the time that should have been filled with me being a hippie, wondering the roads, letting my feet be naked, reading books, practicing yoga, peace & harmony, teaching yoga, meditating and listening to what my inner Divine had to say.

Instead, I found myself climbing the corporate ladder, sad very often, feeling empty with no plan and not really loving where I was. My radiant relationship

with Divine was never given a chance. With new
knowledge came new tools. I started looking up
information online, this world of ordering online and
finding things that were not in my own town, became
my second home. It was also where I found my first
meditation kit. I was ready to start on some sort of
path. I was ready to begin building my relationship
with my Divine.

I had always been an easy child. I could sit for
hours with a pen and paper, in the same spot,
whether other kids were around or not. Sitting still
has never been a problem. So as our courtship began
with a meditation, I had brand new expectations.

Listening to the one you love is of utmost
importance, especially if the relationship is to shine
inside each of you, but I wanted to hear it
immediately. I got antsy and sitting still became
frustrating. All of my life I was taught how to pray
before bed, before meals, when things were bad, even
when they were good, giving thanks and praise.

Meditation was not part of the instruction manual I was handed.

It was hard to learn to sit and listen. For over a year I was a devoted listener for ten minutes a day. I would have a yoga practice, take my final relaxation and then sit up and be still for ten more minutes as a dedication to the Divine. After that year I noticed changes in my life that were what I thought were horrible at the time. But I learned about the cracks in the celling being the conduit for light.

My life wasn't where I wanted it to be, but it was better than it had ever been. I was transitioning from the corporate world to going after my passion. I have dedicated myself to spreading the love of Yoga. I desperately wanted to offer my intuitive healing. However, I realized that ten minutes meditation was not enough for me.

If I expected a radiant relationship with the Divine, I had to put a little more devotion behind it. Not having eight hours of my day cut out to think about Business Administration freed up my time for study. I was now past the honeymoon stage. Those ten minutes a day may have been fun, but now the real work needed to be done.

I started to venture out into the world. With no direction you can only go so far until you get confused. By now my meditation was close to 30 minutes. I had loved the stillness. Sometimes I'd listen to music and sometimes I would listen to nothing.

Sometimes I'd just wait and listen for anything I was supposed to receive. I was diligent. There was a glow kindling between my Divine and me. But it still wasn't where it needed to be. I was seeking some sort of validation.

When you are the only one doing something in your world, not second-guessing yourself is hard. No matter how good I felt, I was holding myself back from my Divine, not even knowing I was doing so. I couldn't fully give my all because I had so many self-limiting, programmed beliefs, hindering me from being authentic.

At the time I didn't know this. But if I had I wouldn't be here. I had no idea what I was looking for, or that I was even looking. But I felt good. Probably could have just lived the rest of my life meditating and been just fine. This time it was my Divine saying, "There is something greater." Blindly I followed my love.

I have been blessed to have four Gurus. I mean truest to the word Gurus, as in one who is responsible for or aids the spiritual growth of another. My Gurus, in a sense, have been our relationship counselors.

I have had many teachers but everyone does. Not many are blessed to have four Gurus. I am thankful for each of them. Upon meeting each of them my radiant relationship with the Divine blossomed into effulgence that is beyond anything I knew existed.

I met my first Guru after applying to teach yoga at a business she managed. I never taught yoga there. But she hasn't stopped teaching me yet. She taught me how to be authentic.

Today it's ok to be me, easy and simple, as long as I act in a righteous manner. Knowing who you are is the only way you can truly know your Divine. Authenticity is something deeper than confidence.

It's a different consciousness of yourself. It's needed in every relationship, especially the one with yourself. By way of my first came two more. These two Gurus changed the course of my spirituality.

They introduced me to affirmations and Sanskrit mantra. Yes I was a yogi, but I hadn't learned that in teacher training. I immediately understood the power of words. What better way to cultivate exactly what you need?! Affirmation and Mantra have been proven over centuries in every religion, to aid in concentration and enhance connection with the Divine.

"Believe and receive" was a common theme from my childhood encounters of the Divine. Many preachers shouted the phrase from the pool pit. Armed with a new tool I stayed focused on my connection, my personal radiant relationship getting closer to my Divine.

Affirmation and Sanskrit mantra led me to chanting; chanting led me to discovering the meaning behind the chants and it has led me to my fourth Guru. She has shown me scriptures that prove I am Divine. I have been told this forever.

Remember I went to church. But the message wasn't received the same way and now I could get it. This connected that final dot that just busted the ceiling wide open. The glass slipper Disney Princess feeling is finally here.

Today my radiant relationship with my Divine is immaculate. I am so in love. There are no conditions and no expectations. All I have to do is be. I am always overwhelmed with an unconditional love that surrounds me. I get so overjoyed sometimes I get emotional, but there is no choir, no church pews, no ushers, only my Divine, me maybe a stone, maybe a mala, maybe a chant maybe not.

Sometimes I talk sometimes I listen. My Divine does the same. We listen to each other and I work daily to become closer connected.

You can now catch my Divine and me holding hands during shavasana at the end of my yoga classes. I see the Divine in everyone more and more daily. I honor it deeply, and there is still something greater that each and every one of us is part of, a radiant relationship with the Divine.

Each of us is different and personal. No matter where you started if you keep the desire of finding your personal truth strong you will always find what's right for you. Your Divine light will lead you to the path of connection and righteousness.

The journey may take a while; you may have to break some chains. If one path doesn't make you feel all frilly foo, find another one.

Keep searching. Finding your connection with the Divine, the divinity in yourself, and in others, keeps you at your natural state of consciousness. One of my Gurus describes this state of consciousness as pure and unconditional love.

There are many paths to achieving this radiant relationship but there is only one destination. Everyone deserves to feel happiness on a celestial level. It is TIME to find your path.

RADIANT RELATIONSHIPS

Be Your Own Hero by Krystalyn Norton

Ever just sit and listen? Really, actually listen.

Taking in with focus the sounds around you…the sound of your own voice. The endless thoughts of the mind…realizing that you are totally alone in the process. There is no one inside your head to hear all the thoughts but you.

Imagine if someone could know you so well…to be so open to your world, that they truly understood you. Imagine the feeling. How it would feel to be truly heard, to have someone get you?

There was this ultimate weapon made by misunderstood housewives called the "point of view gun." All they wanted was to be understood. Isn't that what we all want? Someone to listen to our story and actually comprehend the whole thing. Enjoying and honored by the process of knowing your story, honored by the sharing.

What a relationship that could be. Manifesting endless potential, a hypothetical true union! But alas, there is only you inside that head of yours and no one person could be there with you at all times. So what is a lonely soul to do?

Cultivate that relationship, the most important relationship, and one with yourself.

Take the opportunity, daily, or even from moment to moment to examine the relationship with yourself. What might it be like if you became that ever listening friend? The one who knows you inside and out and is always there for you in the most profound ways.

So when you existing with yourself on a daily basis, what does your internal dialogue sound like? Like a barrage of internal abuse, self-sabotaging comments? Well-grounded realist rationalizations or new age esoteric affirmations?

How honest, down to your core honest, is this dialogue? Are you truly willing to believe in the self or is that trust compromised?

Then just as honestly as you looked inside, watch what appears in your reality. What relationships you have created and what they show you about you, or who you think you are. You might want to sit with this one for a while...or the rest of your life. Becoming ever more conscious of the reality you create.

And what might it feel like to reestablish that true feeling of trust, to nurture your relationship with the unknown? And what would it really be like to step into the grace of courageous introspection? What are you willing to be responsible for?

Imagine a time when you felt totally powerless and a victim of circumstances. Now imagine what your hero would look like and how that hero would make you feel. What if that hero was you your ultimate divine masculine, arriving just in time to save the day!

Can you imagine always knowing, trusting that your knight in shining armor would arrive precisely when he means to, like any great fairy tale? Let's say you have discovered this internal hero, what would his attributes be and how might you cultivate those same attributes?

What percent of your emotional state are you willing to take responsibility for? Say it was 100%. How frighteningly empowering! You actually are responsible for your emotional state. No one else can take on that responsibility, and if you try to pawn it off on another of if they enable you to do so, that said relationship will usually end in disaster.

There are a number of formulas that set the stage, allow you to step out and shift perspectives as well as speaking from an empowering and embodied place. Theses and all other strengthening practices are where the work begins and practice is the key.

To be whole in yourself, taking responsibility for your own emotions and being able to communicate non-violently about what is happening for you with in the context of the relationship. And yet all the while staying connected to the inner stillness, to the field beyond relating to any other. That's a tricky one...comes with practice.

Offer your experience and see what happens. Be open to transformation. So as the Sanskrit chakra name muldahara describes be self-supported! Radiating from the inside out, shining no matter the external circumstances. Communicate your truth, your experience from a clear-grounded place and allow others to do the same by holding the space for that to be shared.

Be generous and be willing to set aside your agenda so that you can truly listen and allow the space for another.

Surrender to your nature of service for each being you interact with, as all are there to reflect for you. See them as they truly are and knowledge the present moment to be the only truth you will ever experience.

Be your own goddess, your own hero. Give yourself that divine union you have always been looking for and the matching vibration will meet you there.

… RADIANT RELATIONSHIPS

Radiance is Created
by Nichole Terry

When I first saw him, he was blowing his damn nose. I thought he was Steve Urkel. If Steve Urkel was chubbier and wearing a striped polo shirt. It was my first summer home from college, and I was staying with a long-term friend after a serious altercation with my father.

I told my friend that I would go out to dinner with him and his two friends after his mother convinced me that it would do me some good to leave the house with "three good looking young men." So, I conceded and agreed to go with them to Chili's. Not the sexiest of places, but at least, I would be able to get out of the house.

All of this led to me now standing in the small entry-way to my friend's mobile home, staring in disbelief at this person who was one pocket protector short of being cast in the remake of Revenge of the Nerds. At that time, I didn't notice the broad shoulders, the great lips, the big heart or the ridiculous IQ, I just looked at him for a long while, and chuckled a little inside while thinking: how stereotypically hilarious.

I don't know how I ended up riding with him to Chili's, but somewhere between the Will Smith's rapping, the awkward dinner, and our long conversation, something began to happen. Most people would have called it chemistry, or love at first site. I called it losing my mind.

I had no cell phone and no car that summer. But I memorized his number the first time he recited it to me. He was completing an engineering internship up the street, and came by the house several times a week to hang out with me. I will never forget the little BP gas station around the corner, and the orange slushies we would get every time we spent time together.

He was a very sweet guy. Honest, considerate, and listened for hours. This was great, because I could talk for hours. I realized I was falling for him, but I fought myself the whole way. He wasn't my type. I liked alpha males and men who could bench me with their pinky finger. I liked athletic men, and the first time I saw him dribble a basketball, I almost lost consciousness from laughing so hard.

But it was what it was, and it took me ten years to learn how to love him, and love myself enough to allow myself to love him, but by then, he wasn't sure if he wanted to even put up with me.

It took ten years because I was a shallow, immature young girl who was more preoccupied with my imaginary idea of myself, and how I thought I wanted others to see me. I allowed my past negative experiences with men (including my father) to dictate the way I related to him, and allowed my friends to make fun of him and thus, negatively affect my view of him.

You know how your girlfriends can be. We think that they are doing their best to look out for us, but sometimes, they are really just bitter, sexually frustrated people who wish they had what you had.

We are all looking for love. But are we really ready to receive it? I believe that I was lucky. I fell in love with a man that I didn't know was the man of my dreams.

And after ten years of dating him on and off, pushing him away, and then chasing him around while he ran for dear life; he gave me a final chance after he realized that I had matured into a less aggressive person who wouldn't bite his head off anymore.

But as I matured, I realized that what I truly wanted and needed at twenty-eight wasn't anything close to what I thought I wanted and needed when I was nineteen. It took almost a decade of nightmare dates, horrendous online encounters, and awful advice from others to understand that maybe, I wasn't doing this right.

I had to realize that it wasn't him that needed to change, it was me. I understood that there were three things I had to do to eventually end up at this blissful point in my life; I just wish that I understood these three things years ago; but better late than never.

1. Stop Putting Yourself Down.

I have never been a small woman, but I used to be a healthy and gorgeous size in high school. However, my father didn't think so, and was consistently pressuring me to lose weight and commenting on my appearance.

This shredded my self-esteem and resulted in a promiscuous college career and a manifestation of binge eating disorder. Unfortunately, this resulted in extremely low self-care, and self-consideration; and I eventually began to believe that I wasn't worthy of being loved.

Now, my partner tries to inform me that he loves me for more than my appearance, but his words mostly fall on deaf ears. My low self-esteem is an ongoing daily fight that began almost fifteen years ago. I know in my heart that I deserve to be loved, but in my head, I still don't believe it, and have to coach myself through this pain daily.

As women, we have grown up hearing and seeing the expectations for us from the media, our parents, our friends and others. If the *Victoria's Secret, Hardees* and *Go Daddy* commercials haven't made it clear enough, I'll reiterate it here.

Tiny waist, huge boobs, long hair, trim hips, petite, feminine, horny and ready to put out at a moment's notice. You see it everywhere and it's annoying, but there's hope.

The media and others don't accurately represent the opinion of all of the men on this earth, and if you're shooting for the attention of douchebag men who only care about how you look, you need to redirect your focus to begin with. If you have large hips, flaunt them, if your breasts aren't that big, who cares?

If you're carrying a few extra pounds, guess what, most people are. If you're taller than most men, it can be guaranteed that someone will love you enough to want to climb up there and sweep you off your feet. You have to realize that you deserve the best. You are unique, and exceptional regardless of your outward appearance, and love isn't just for the "lucky or the strong." You can have it too.

As women, we need to do what it takes to fight for our self-esteem and develop a positive self-view. If your self-esteem has been taking hits for years, as in my personal experience, look into speaking with a counselor or working with others who have had the same challenges.

Do everything you can to spend more time with yourself, learn who you truly are, and what your heart's desire is. Form a strong relationship with yourself, and understand your value. When we understand our value, and stop putting ourselves down, we are less likely to form toxic relationships, and thus leave room in our lives for radiant and loving ones.

2. Stop Selling Yourself Short.

During the pitiable dating escapades that took place after the man I loved called off our relationship, I realized my affinity for exceedingly muscular men. Now being a plus-sized girl, I happily welcomed the attention of several physically arousing men, even though I knew in my heart that there was no way in hell we would make it past a few months of fun.

But because I was not happy with my appearance, and had never been accepted by my father (paging Dr. Freud, line one), I felt lucky to have the attention of men ranging from Army Rangers, and dumb gym rats, to a club bouncer who looked like Dwayne Johnson; who I am embarrassed to say, is my celebrity crush and believe me it was HARD not to tackle this look-alike where he stood.

But I soon found out that well-formed pectorals, and huge biceps were not enough to sustain a loving and radiant relationship. And I also realized that 90% of my standards for love weren't being met.

I had to realize that I deserved the attention of a man who met all of my standards and not just men who met my physical ones. As women, we are told by our girlfriends and other women in our lives that we need to lower our standards and just find a "good man." What constitutes a "good man" has changed over time, but now it mostly consists of someone who has some sort of a job, a car that runs and wants to commit…eventually.

Unfortunately, however, cheating numerous times, having a criminal record and the inability to relate to you and others without violent tendencies tends to get thrown out of the window, as long as we have him and he pays for a few things, or his bedroom abilities have resulted in several followup chiropractic visits.

Here's the truth; stop selling yourself short. If he doesn't meet your needs, keep it moving. Make a list of what are the most important qualities you want in your partner, and set your sights on those who represent those qualities.

Don't deviate from your list, or you will find out that your relationship status on Facebook will always be "complicated." We all love orgasms and attention, but if you can't find the right person to give those things to you now; buy a vibrator and get a puppy.

You deserve an excellent, loving relationship, so stop wasting your time on losers, stop selling yourself short and increase your chances of having a radiant relationship.

3. Stop Listening to Your Friends and Everyone Else.

This step has been briefly mentioned in the previous ones, but deserves its own separate section because it is extremely important. If you want to have a radiant relationship that is enjoyable, fulfilling, uplifting and all that you want it to be; you have to stop taking advice from your family, friends, *Steve Harvey, Oprah, Ted Talks,* your boss, your secretary, your mailman, your pastor, your children, *Cosmo Girl, Dr. Phil, Real Housewives, Fifty Shades of Grey*, Jennifer Lopez movies and everything else.

All of this input is confusing and somewhat ridiculous, and 99% of it doesn't even apply to you or your unique situation.

I will never forget when Steve Harvey's book *Act Like a Lady, Think Like a Man* came out. Like most single, briefly celibate, twenty-something, African American women, I bought the book and read it. While some of the advice was helpful, I found the rest of it contradictory, confusing and disheartening.

My general understanding of the book was this: men are sex crazed, inconsiderate dogs who need to be tricked and trained into loving you.

The most memorable piece of advice from the book was to, "Wait 90 days before sleeping with your new man." This was particularly confusing because if I was supposed to "think like a man" then I'm really not supposed to wait 90 minutes before sleeping with my date.

But if I'm supposed to "act like a lady," then I'm supposed to run around in circles and make him chase me until I get a ring, which will probably take longer than 90 days.

It all seemed frankly ridiculous. So put down the book and realized that this advice, and a lot of other "love advice" had nothing to do with me, who I was, and what I wanted in my relationship. If I wanted to be happy with anyone, I needed to stop listening to the rampant opinions of others and stick with what I knew I wanted.

If you find yourself single and ready to mingle, but you're not sure how to do so because of the influx of input from others; stop listening to them. You know what you want, and you know what's best for you. As women, we have to learn to trust ourselves and our desires.

There will always be information available from loved ones and others regarding how to form and maintain a radiant relationship, but most of this is based on their personal experiences, and is now mostly muddled by bitterness or a broken heart. So be cautious when accepting other's input regarding your love life, and trust yourself more than you trust them.

Ten years ago, when standing in the entry way of my friend's mobile home, I had no idea that I was going to fall in love with the awkward boy blowing his nose. I ignored my feelings of attraction, and spent a decade allowing other's opinions to dictate how I saw myself, and how I saw him.

I put myself down, and sold myself short. I wouldn't allow myself to love him, and I wouldn't allow myself to love me.

It took me ten years to learn to break these horrible habits. But now, even though I still have a long way to go, I am enjoying an amazingly radiant and incredibly loving relationship with the very man I had no idea was my perfect fit. I learned it wasn't impossible to find love, I did deserve it and not only is my relationship radiant, but my life is too.

This reality can be anyone's who desires to have it. Radiance is created, not forced. So turn off *Dr. Phil*, quit listening to your mother, pour a glass of wine and watch *Scandal,* radiant love is not far away.

RADIANT RELATIONSHIPS

Radiant Relationship with Myself:
Fourteen Steps I Followed for Healing and Self-Love Recovery After Depression and Anxiety
by Kiki Dombrowski

My entire life has been dotted with periods of severe depression and anxiety: some periods last only a couple of weeks, while others last for months. Sometimes the depression is manageable, while other times it was so debilitating that I could not even muster the energy to go to work. I am not a doctor.

I did not spend hours in the book racks of the psychology library to piece together this essay. I do not hold a doctoral degree in neuroscience. Instead, what I have chosen to do in this essay is share my personal methods for healing and recovery after a serious period of anxiety and depression so I could return to having a healthy and loving relationship with myself.

I have identified some specific methods and mantras which have helped me through the most difficult times, helped me repair my outlook on the future as well as restore my faith in the present process of observation, sensation, and healing. The steps do not necessarily belong in a concrete sequential order, though I find they naturally occurred for me in the structure I set forward in this essay.

As a result, the essay follows my personal journey through the healing process and self-love recovery I faced after experiencing my most recent period of depression and anxiety, which proved to be one of the most challenging.

My hope is that in sharing these steps, I am able to help others who may have gone through, or are going through, similar personal challenges, and in doing so, recognize that there is hope and opportunity for growth and an awareness so strong and brilliant, that a radiant relationship within the self is worth fighting for.

1. I am allowed to cry. The first step for releasing anxiety, depression, and other challenging emotions has been through the process of crying. Crying can be incredibly healing, both physically and emotionally. In *The Health Benefit of Tears,* Dr. Judith Orloff said she smiled when patients cried because they were courageously healing depression or other difficult emotions with tears. I have found crying to be just that: courageous healing. Crying has allowed me to release stress, anxiety, sadness, and the heaviness I feel in my body from those challenging emotions. I have learned to accept that crying can be cathartic, and that it is okay to cry for as long as necessary and wherever necessary. The question I ask myself: How does crying help or hinder me during periods of anxiety and depression?

2. I ask for help. Anxiety and depression are serious illnesses to have to endure, and no one should be expected to go through it alone. It can be incredibly difficult finding a therapist to be compatible with, but the effort to find that therapist is necessary in overcoming many hurdles in anxiety and depression. I had to ask myself many questions:

Do I want to see a therapist, and if so, what kind? Do I want to try medications, or other forms of medicinal treatment- if so, what are the possible side effects? In addition to seeking counseling and therapy, there may be underlying causes or concerns that trigger depression.

For me, I struggled with finances while looking for a full-time job. Money was a major trigger for anxiety. I had to ask for financial help, even though it was difficult for me to do so because I had to overcome being too proud to reach out for assistance. Asking for help comes in many forms, and I found that the support and comfort of people's aid in itself was comforting and healing. The question I ask myself: Have I reached out to all possible resources of treatment for my anxiety and depression?

3. I allow myself space from others when I need to be alone. Being alone can offer a time to find peace and quiet, as opposed to the distracting or hectic nature of constantly being surrounded by others. Sometimes social interactions feel overwhelming in the midst of anxiety and depression. I am a very strong introvert and tend to find being in large groups of people or noisy and busy social situations (loud concerts or big parties, for example) to be draining and awkward.

It would feel like I couldn't communicate clearly, that there was a distinct energetic separation between myself and others. I would frequently make the comment that I felt "like a foreigner on planet Earth." When I felt like that, I found being around others to be depleting: my discomfort and disconnection would feel amplified by the fact that I didn't relation to others, additionally causing my confidence to plummet.

The awkwardness and discomfort I felt were red flags that it was time to retreat into my own space and briefly distance myself from social situations and large groups of people. By stepping out of the social limelight, I was able to turn the attention inwards and focus on relationship with myself. The energy I would have spent on keeping up with other people was then redirected towards working on taking care of myself. The question I ask myself: How can I make my time alone a beneficial and healing experience?

4. I confide in those who support and love me.
It seems to contrast to the last step; however, there are times we wish to retreat and there are times we wish to reach out. I have a web of people who I have depended on for comfort, laughter, joy, and emotional support.

I found that sharing what I was going through with the friends and family I trusted not only helped me heal, but also helped our bond grow stronger. My friends and family could see me vulnerable and could be there to help me feel better. Most importantly, I let my friends and family know how much they mean to me, thanking them for being an important part of my life. The question I ask myself: Who is there to love me unconditionally and be willing to listen to me when I need to express myself?

5. I rest when my body tells me to. Dealing with

depression and anxiety can be physically and mentally exhausting. I found I would continually force myself through events and obligations, considering them responsibilities I'd committed myself to being present for.

For me, exhaustion felt like ten steps beyond being tired. I was irritable, confused, and offended easily. Even though I was tired, I still couldn't sleep properly, either because I had nightmares or couldn't have restful sleep.

The truth is: the number one responsibility and obligation in my life was to redirect my attention back to myself and understanding my own body's limitations in times of mental suffering. So when I was tired, I cancelled plans and removed as many stressful obligations from my life. I also slept when I needed to, honoring nights that I slept extra hours and daytime naps that helped me push through the rest of the day.

I considered the time I was sleeping time my body could recuperate, heal, and curb stress and depression. If I had problems with tossing and turning, I would put a couple drops of lavender and peppermint oil on my pillow. I would also try a chamomile tea with a few drops of passionflower extract in it. Sometimes I would even put on my headphones and listen to binaural beats.

Any way I could, I would give myself extra rest while suffering depression, just as I would give myself extra rest when I had the flu. The result was feeling of having more energy when I was awake allowed me to keep focused on tasks longer and also helped me stay in a better mood longer. The question I ask myself: What does mindful resting mean to me, and how do I commit to giving myself mindful rest?

6. I learn to breathe and smile. Seems simple enough, but in the darkest of moments it feels almost patronizing when someone: says to you Chin up! However, cheering up through the small physical steps of breathing and smiling is something I try to remind myself of, whether I have a small moment of stress or think I am going to tumble into a major meltdown.

I take deep breaths, and if I can muster it: I try and smile, even a little bit. Smiling can reduce stress, and it is hard to stay angry or upset when you are smiling. After a while, you are not faking a smile, you are just smiling. The questions I ask myself: Can I pause right now to breathe in deeply and slowly? Can I hold a smile for ten seconds?

7. I recall the blessings in my life. Sometimes it is hard to see clearly through the darkness and heaviness of anxiety and depression. Honestly, I found that there were some days where I could not manage to come up with a simple list of blessings, not because they were not there, but because my mind could not access them.

Because of this, I had three things that I was grateful for that I would return to: my dog, my boyfriend, and my siblings. On other days, I could create a list of three things easily, based on events that were occurring around me: For example: I am grateful for the chance to take a long hike on this sunny day, I am grateful I have the money to pay my bills this week, I am grateful I have the opportunity to cook a favorite dinner tonight.

Either way, I found this practice allows me to change my perspective: instead of focusing on the negatives or tuning in to the critical inner voice, I turn my attention to what was positive in my life. The blessings I considered were beacons of hope and focus points as I moved through the process of healing, allowing me to have something healthy to turn my internal conversation towards. The question I ask myself: What are three things in my life that I am grateful for at this given moment?

8. I put my body in motion when I feel the need to be productive. A common side effect of depression is the feeling of lethargy, as discussed earlier. There were times I could not do much moving around, opting for sleep and rest over action and activity. But at other points I felt the need to be active and use the energy that was returning to my body.

I did anything I felt motivated to do to get me up and moving around such as simply yoga positions, hiking or walking in the woods, cooking, or a visit to the sauna. Doing any of these things felt like major accomplishments, as I was using my time to better myself and my well-being. It had my circulation flowing and my mind awake and aware of my physical body. The question I ask myself: What physical activities do I like to do to get me up and moving?

9. I engage in creative activities and productive hobbies. Expression through creative activities is one of the most beneficial ways to explore emotions, personality traits, and artistic talents. When I was in my darkest hour, I couldn't even relate to the hobbies I once loved. Writing seemed like the hardest challenge: I could no longer hear the dialogue of articles or chapters play out in my mind. I was starting to come out of the dark end of my struggle with depression when I wanted to return to the hobbies and activities that I always loved. I made a daily ritual of writing, whether I recorded a dream in my journal, wrote a poem, or made a small revision to an article I was working on. Any creative activity can make the difference between feeling unproductive or feeling proactively inspired. Whether writing a story, baking a cake, knitting a scarf, or reading a new book, creative activities brightened my spirit. The question I ask myself: What engaging activities and hobbies allow me to explore my interests and express myself creatively?

10. I reclaim the present moment. I was once told you feel depression when you are thinking about a past you can't change. You feel anxiety when you are thinking about a future that has not happened yet. I have related to this saying on countless occasions, especially when I started to feel I was panicking.

When my thoughts were out of control, I found the panic came not from living in the present moment, but worrying about something in either the past or the future. Either way, they were thoughts and events that I either manifested in my imagination or were events that occurred completely out of my control.

To detour my thoughts into more optimistic routes, I did the following: If I found myself worrying about what was going to happen in the future, I would tell myself the most benevolent outcome. If I found myself brooding over a decision I made in the past, I would tell myself, everything happens for a reason.

I would try to go back to the deep breathing, as I found I could focus on my breath slowly moving in and out, and the focus on the breath constantly keeping me in the present moment. I would also take a moment to observe my surroundings, focusing on what was right in front of me. The question I ask myself: What do I observe about my present surroundings and what captivates me about this current atmosphere?

11. I explore spirituality and what faith means to me. This is not a call to be a devout or fervent religious person, but a reminder for myself to return to spirit. When I was depressed I struggled with feeling like I didn't belong anywhere, that sense of feeling comfort and security was not accessible, unless I tried to access divinity.

Divinity to me represents the great mystery of the creator, the divine spark to ignite our universe into being. Connecting with divinity allowed me to feel a sense of belonging, peace, and faith. I could simply ask Goddess/God/Creator/Great Divine to direct and guide me.

I explored spirituality through a number of avenues: the most valuable being the holiday celebrations I spend with a group of Druids. In solitary moments I practiced meditation and chanting. There were also the times I simply looked upwards into the night sky and focused on specific constellations contemplating the vastness of the universe, trying to remind myself that I belonged to a place of abundance, expansion, creation, and mystery.

The exploration of spirituality and faith is one of the most valuable methods for healing and relief, knowing that divinity was not only an outward sensation, but an internal one as well. The questions I ask myself: How does being spiritual feel? How does divinity reveal itself to me?

12. I forgive others and practice compassion. I found this, and find this, to be one of the more difficult of steps for me to practice. One of my finest and most challenging qualities is that I am sensitive, but as a result, often emotionally affected and oftentimes offended by the actions of those around me.

It is not that I am a cynical person by nature, but I do get easily flustered in social situations as a result of my anxiety. I have always had a problem with personalizing what other people do. Someone would cut me off in traffic, and I would think, "Why did that jerk do that to me?" The truth is, that person cutting me off did not do that to upset or offend me. That person was stressed and under pressure to get somewhere quickly, or just maybe, was a lousy driver.

When I found myself being short with others, or responding in an unsavory way, I realized I needed to slow down my reaction rate and stop my mind from racing. I'd first ask myself if I was overreacting. I then tried to resolve negative thoughts and I forgave the person for hurting my feelings. I tried to practice perspective, wondering what if that person was going through what I was going through?

I would send them thoughts of love and healing: I had one client tell me that when she felt anger towards another person-maybe they were rude or acted in a way she did not agree with, she would visualize herself through Happy Fairy Dust on them. The other method for feeling compassion for me is simply doing good deeds for others with zero expectations.

I would pay for the person's coffee behind me in line at the coffee shop. I oftentimes offer free tarot readings online. I collect canned food to bring to a homeless shelter. However, a small the act of gratitude could create a motion of bigger acts of gratitude, changing people's days for the better so more people feel a warmth and patience for those around them.

The questions I ask myself: How would you react if that person were a close friend or family member? What can you do to make that persons day better?

13. I identify and express healthy self-talk. It can be a challenging exercise for someone with depression or anxiety to identify different aspects of his/her personality that he/she truly values. When I felt depressed and anxious, I could not find very many things I loved about myself, turning to negative self-talk.

It was a toxic form of self-abuse that distorted the way I saw myself physically and well as well destroying my relationship with myself. When I started to push through the depression and come out the other side, I realized that part of the healing process would involve identifying things I love about myself. Instead of falling into a spiral of critical and abusive self-talk, I spent time considering personality traits I liked about myself.

When I thought about how powerful my mind was, even in the grips of depression and anxiety, I was quite impressed with my level of brightness. It was the starting point for healthy self-talk for me when I was able to say, I have such a unique and powerful mind, it has allowed me to have an incredible ability of observation, research, and insight.

Following this pattern, I worked to identify different aspects about myself that I loved. I expressed the value of these aspects to myself, establishing a healthier relationship with myself. When I expressed healthy self-talk to myself, my confidence and self-worth began to return. The questions I ask myself: What is it about me that is special? What about me is valuable?

14. I revisit, revise, and plan short term and long-term goals. This is a monumental shift in thinking, as it shows going from a place of despair to a place of hope. When motivation returns and the energy to see projects through no longer feel foreign, it feels like having successfully climbed an emotional mountain, having travelled through the various stages of recovering from depression and anxiety.

By planning goals, I have a sense of hope and a sense that there is so much to look forward to. By setting both short term and long-term goals I also know that I can feel a sense of satisfaction and accomplishment soon as well as in the future. The questions I ask myself: What goal would make me proud to complete today? What goal would make me proud to complete this week? Which goals would make me proud to complete in the next year?

RADIANT RELATIONSHIPS

The Stormwall by Jessie Jean Damico

Compassionately naïve and much too frivolous with my precious heart, I felt trapped in our marriage. It was a home-grown human-conditioned hell. We were complicated hostages of our own devices, unsettled on our parents' laurels, stunted in our individual self-discovery.

While he focused on blame, I sought harmony and the flow. Nonetheless, in a house of love, we were triggers for each other.

How courageous was our love? How could I hold open the sacred space for him to heal from his past, while it was being projected at me? How could I remain compassionately open-hearted, when his outdated coping mechanisms were breaking my heart and pushing me further and further away?

Even with external help, how could our love withstand the mounting toxicity brewing between us?

He was not a broken man, but rather, he was a haunted one. And I was the scapegoat his ghosts called Pollyanna. Essentially, the innate desire to see the good, even in our dysfunctional situation, was unyieldingly devastating.

We were drowning in a living death, because it was the only way we knew how to survive, to make it work. I was starving for acceptance, shouting to be heard, begging for understanding, seeking companionship in a lonely/hollow relationship and co-morbidly loyal through the dysfunction of it all.

I gave and he took…I fought for scraps. Perhaps, he never really loved me; maybe, he never really could. Was this even love? Should love be this difficult?

At all costs, I tried to believe in his rhetorical empty promises, as well as his potential. But his guarded heart's selfish intentions kept giving the truth away. How much longer could I survive in denial?

How much longer was I willing to sacrifice my integrity to remain in this unhealthy relationship? Even though he liked the way my love made him feel, it was not enough to resuscitate our vows.

It could only get as bad as I allowed it to. And after hitting the bottom and falling through it, I reached my limit. The little girl inside refused to stand in favor of her own demise. My inner child stopped hoping for his hand, for his open heart.

So, in pieces and tears, on the cold kitchen floor of our home, the rose-colored glasses were foregone. I found my voice and began to speak my truth.

For the first time in my life, I put myself first. Resultantly, our "forever" became terminal. Soon after, we carried our broken hearts and wounded egos over the threshold of divorce. At the beginning and end if it all, you know your heart and he knows his. Accepting the truth may take lifetimes.

AWAKENING

Struck by lightning, the day the he filed for divorce, I will never be the same again. On the day he told me that he filed, it was as if I just "woke up." An "aha" moment traveling on a discrete path through the Great Unknown torched the dream with concussive force. In an instant, the Maya of this world was torn away.

My ex-husband absconded, dragging the kite-tail illusion of our life together behind him. He never looked back, never apologized for deserting our marriage and taking all we built and all our dreams with him. Everything I thought I knew was obscuring from view. If not real, it seemed to disappear.

Consequently, I began my transition. I shed my skin to free my spirit. My naked soul began to burn in furious flames of unrequited love. Raw and broken, scattered in puddles on the floor, I took a deep breath, the first breath, initiating the journey, back home to the heart of self. The tears of pain and relief began to pour.

SURRENDER

For so long, I was so strong. Nevertheless, when I fell through the paper world my mirage of a marriage was fecundated on, the past oxidized superfluously in the parallel-like dimensions of grief and loss.

So, somewhere between here and there, broken down, stranded on the side of the road, in the middle of nowhere, in darkest of the night, all by myself, finally, I surrendered.

Despairingly, I relinquished the counterfeit sense of control over that which was out of my control. As I raised my arms to the constellations and surrendered to the fates, I hoped for a response.

Contemporaneously, a compassionately weathered man showed up singing his own song. Akin to a knight in rickety tin armor with a heart painted on his sleeve, he came to my rescue.

Perhaps out of his own need or habit, like a cigarette, he lit the dimming embers of my heart aflame. Earnestly, he rekindled my faith in Love. Then, he drove me home.

Home was a family who took me in like an abandoned and left-for-dead kitten in the tundra of divorce. With unconditional empathy, they fed me, loved me, and nurtured me back to heart. They kept me safe and warm as I battered through the remainder of my storm.

Certainly, there is a sacred freedom in an act of sensuous surrender. When we surrender, we can experience the beautiful totality life is. Everyone and everything we need will come to us at the right time. And each moment holds a decipherable lesson. Be open and receptive.

REBIRTH

Heartbreak can be a raw initiation for deeper love and wisdom, a symbolic rebirth of the authentic self.

Yet, the pain of one's heart breaking open can be excruciating. I was a rag doll left for dead in the morning fog, torn and crowning through the stitches and seams, at the dawn of my new life. With each mournful contraction, I could hear my soul being called to evolve.

For love, I did not lose myself, as many do. In loving, I may have dulled myself to stay with him. I may have drowned my intuition to disregard the truth. I may have weighted myself down with his baggage to give him the opportunity to grow his dreams and feel his happiness. But I never lost myself.

Instead, the world I once found myself living in was lost. Overnight, it all faded away. So clear in the light of my soul is my heart's truth. This new beginning commences at the end of the tunnel. I must travel through the grief to be reborn into who I am.

THE WEEPING WILLOW

Grief

The severance of the unbalanced love between lovers is a subconsciously invited death of the ego and a renaissance of validity. So, I began to teeter between mourning and rejoicing respectfully in melancholy waves of grief and ecstatic.

With terrible bouts of emotional incontinence, I came to realize heartbreak as a viral illness. Accordingly, in pursuance of healing, I let grief run its course. The symptoms included the following: Denial, Anger, Bargaining, Depression, and Acceptance.

Stages of grief can move in any order, in any combination, for any duration of time. I was as prepared as possible and went with the flow. It came in dreadful, rippling waves that will forever affect the landscape of this life.

At times, moments seemed to pass as eons. When the promise of forever died, time ceased to exist, at least for a little while. In those instances, loneliness carved caverns in the spaces between soul and skin.

It felt like a violent stabbing, an etching of abysmal emptiness. Yet, I was not alone, really. We never are.

It was an occasion to reach out for support. I wanted to seek those who offered encouragement, empowerment, hope and humor. However, for a while, I did not tell anyone what was going on. Part of me thought I could handle it on my own.

Another part was embarrassed. And really, after all these years, I did not know how to ask for help.

Since my breaking heart felt no hunger and had no need to dream, I was not eating, hardly sleeping. I was withering away, surrounded by empty moving boxes and nowhere to go. In the midst of dismay, I fell apart.

Yet, it felt so amazing, so beautiful to be alive and to have loved so deeply that I could be as broken as I was. Nonetheless, I needed help, guidance, and reassurance.

"The Sisterhood"

At the end of a yoga class, one of my students, a (Super) women, a friend, asked me how I was losing so much weight, so quickly. She was concerned, she wondered if I was getting sick. Uncomfortably, I made a joke about how I never knew how much my diamond ring weighed, then showed her my naked left hand from which it was missing.

Humor may have saved my life that night. After class, she took me out to dinner and we talked and listened for hours.

She shared her similar story and without judgment, listened to mine. We acknowledged one another's feelings. Through sharing stories, much of the pain was released.

Also, she welcomed me to what she called the "Sisterhood," a supportive community of collective understanding and unconditional love on the path towards healing, a reminder to lift others as I climb.

This friend was one of a few special people who helped me on the braided path of divorce recovery and self-(re)-discovery.

Further along this path, with a curative birthday kiss, my reflection showed up. And he kept showing up. This mirror showed me how much I have grown, endured, and how much fun life can be when we free ourselves from expectations and live in love.

In my reflection, I found my wings and learned to soar like an eagle above the remainder of the storm.

Languishingly, I reconnected with old friends and reached out to family members. This was vital in coping. Together, we reconnected with the commonality of our roots and the sacredness of love.

Not only were these friends and relatives invested in my well-being, they also knew me by heart. They reminded me of who I was before this bellowing maelstrom through marital bliss, chaos, crisis, divorce, and recovery.

Keep in mind, every person is a lesson. What are they teaching us? When they speak listen from the heart. Everyone we encounter is on their own journey, as well. What is our role in their journey? When they listen, speak from the heart.

Distractions

In addition to connecting with others who understood, distractions were helpful, too. When thoughts got too heavy, I set them down. Instead of getting lost in the mind and all its insecurities and what-ifs, I went dancing.

On the dance floor, I was set free. And in the spaces between the music, I reencountered suspended elements of self and thawed them back into the biorhythm of my beating heart.

Movement to exercise my grieving thoughts and grave emotions helped me progress through this bewildering time. With intention and need, I began a running meditation. Up and down the winding, back-country dirt roads, I would inhale peace and calm, acceptance and forgiveness.

Then, I exhaled pain, lies, anger, etc. It really helped me cope. With each step and stride, I was beginning to surrender once again and more completely into the flow.

Plus, to help myself through this incomprehensibly unrefined shift, I took up hobbies, both old and new. After all these years, of dimming my light to let those I love shine, the creative light inside began to saturate the tabula rasa canvas of this new life. I began to paint from the flow of my heart and soul.

If ever I was expressive, I was the most amid the enlightenment of grief. I began a poetry blog. I got a journal and wrote it all down. Once on paper, it was out of me. Journaling was a healthy means to expressing grief.

Grieving can be daring and expansive, too. Learning to play the piano challenged my brain. When primarily focused on the piano, my screaming thoughts were percussively drowned out.

Fearlessly, alone or in the company of kindred friends, I went whitewater rafting, explored waterfalls, and climbed a mountain in the middle of the night just to watch the sun rise at its peak.

Grieve but do not remain stagnant out of fear. You will get through this. Think of it as an opportunity to grow and learn. Honor your broken heart. Be patient with yourself through the process.

THE JOURNEY

Healing

The unmovable mover, the mountain becomes grains of sand beneath the feet of men and women journeying towards healing and self-(re)discovery. As I drove away, exiled from the life I chose, through cracks in closed blinds and locked doors, my ex-husband and the skeletons and ghosts he was hiding with watched.

As the glittering light left the cabin on the hill, this scene became just another tragic Stockholm rerun playing in the background.

In the company of my dog riding shotty, I embarked with patience and tenderness on this introspective adventure. It took courage to leave the familiar, to inaugurate this journey into fearless authenticity, called adulthood.

My car was packed with moving boxes and bags of baggage. Our first stop was the garbage dump. There we disposed of the edges of our emotional belongings.

Next, and with assistance, I cached most of the remaining items into a storage unit, to be organized at a later date. I was astonished to see how my entire life thus far fit into a minimal-sized pod. My whole life was in limbo tethered to this margin as my laundry was aired for all to judge.

The Nest

With a desperate and open heart, I visited psychic. She directed me to a venue, a nursery of stars. Wherein, I would find a safe-haven to hide and a parliament of awakened pilgrims to heal and grow amongst.

I would have spent lifetimes and traveled the globe seeking my ageless nomadic tribe of kindred spirits. Together, we mucked through many existential dilemmas of the human condition, nursing similar wounds. This whisper in the wind guiding me to them in my time of need was a blessing.

As the storm winds dwindled, the breeze blew through the holes in my heart. I fluttered like a feather into a strawberry field. In the field, there was an oak tree and high in its branches I saw a steppingstone. It appeared as an inviting nest to gather my thoughts and pieces.

This life of unbecoming is meant to help us to develop into our true self. This was a time for changes and choices, not rules…a path to a new, independent beginning. The next nine months were spent on an introspective colonoscopic journey into self. It took time to process all that had occurred.

Healing is not found in geography, necessarily. It is found inside yourself and those attempting to help you. Through contact, we are transformed. When people open their hearts, they heal. Allow your scars to fall in love.

The devastation of divorce can become a profound transformation. We always have a choice. Choose to be the survivor rather than the victim. As we overcome toxic emotions and begin to open ourselves to the gifts of a new life, embrace its lessons of wholeness and serenity.

It is healthy to leave controlling relationships for loving ones instead. When it was time to move on to the next stepping stone, I packed my purple backpack, closed the door and left through the open window.

As I packed my car full of my plants, the sky opened up and I was caught in a sun shower washing me clean of the abusive cyclical patterns of my past.

Forgiveness

Life can be cruel. Sometimes we make bad choices. Loving my ex-husband was the most self-destructive thing I have ever known and committed to. The worst thing I did was stay too long.

For nearly 13 years, I bled my patience, love, time, and self into helping my husband. Because he asked me to, I gave more. Because he needed me to, I forgave him for running my well dry and rarely fulfilling his promises to nurture and emotionally support me in my endeavors.

Since the dysfunction in our relationship was familiar to me, from my past, I put my dreams on the back burner. I lived and died on Plan B.

A few months before he fled our home and filed for divorce in secrecy, and upon our joint agreement, I handed my letter of resignation to the principal of the school I was teaching at. Together, my ex and I were in a position, for me to begin transitioning into living my Plan A life with him.

That meant, for the first time in 13 years, I would need to depend on him for support, both emotional and financial. Principally, this was all part of our initiated plan. Shortly after I began transitioning from Plan B to Plan A, he left "us."

After all those years of my dedication and support to our team, he left me with nearly nothing. What an ungluing plot twist…

Never was it a matter of who he left me for. Whether he left me for a man or woman, his mother or a younger dame, he still left. Despite everything, the last thing I said to my ex-husband was, "I am sorry for my part. I love you. And I hope you heal." Unfortunately, there is no prize for being the bigger person.

Or was there? Ironically, the most loving-like thing he may have ever done for me was leave. I can only hope he did it out of love/like and not out of shame, guilt, or vengeance. As time has distanced me from the most painful of emotions and the fog begins to clear into mid-life, I start to see more objectively.

When people we love are sick, sometimes loving them from afar is the only thing we can do to protect ourselves from losing ourselves as they lose their minds. To begin truly healing from this heartbreak, I needed to view him as unstable and immature as he truly was and forgive him for his actions, or lack thereof.

Even more difficult than forgiving him was forgiving myself for giving him so much of my time, life, love, and effort. It was very difficult to accept that I allowed and invited my ex-husband to treat me the way he did, for as long as I did. For the most part, at any time, I could have walked away, but I stayed.

In retrospect, it was an unhealthy love. I had to let it go. He may have a beautiful heart, but it needed to be open to me for healthy love to grow between us. Someone who really loved me would have wanted to help me grow and become my best self.

I made a mistake. When we make mistakes, it just means we were wrong. We were being human, perfectly imperfect people. I did not know then what I know now. I will never make this mistake again. Eventually I dug up this deeper truth and forgave myself for this.

In spite of everything, all we can do is live, love, and learn. We cannot go back, nor can we change the past. However, we can accept it, forgive ourselves and others for it, and learn from it. When you find peace within yourself, you will love and forgive yourself.

In this dim light of familiarity, you will know when you are ready to evolve and transform...

Self-Love

Honor your intuition, always. Intuition comes from within; it is your soul speaking through your heart. Permit self-love to carry you like the ocean when you first learn to float.

Be yourself. Well, more accurately, allow yourself to be yourself. Live every kind of life. Dream every kind of dream. Believe in your life and your dreams. Our lives are worth our time, invest in yourself. Discover who you are and the truth of your being.

Love the miracle who is you.

True self-love is acceptance of oneself. Take your time. Follow your heart. Sometimes following your heart means losing your mind. Get out of your head and live from your heart, instead.

The most important relationship we have in life is with the self. Nurture this bond into bloom. Recognize your day to day cadence; it is the ebb and flow of your life. There are so many lives within this waking life, take time to rediscover and redefine you.

Fall in love with yourself and then the natural process of growing together with another will follow…

Humble Bees

Divorce will change you. Let it humble you, rather than make you bitter. Either way, you will see the world differently than before. Considering all that was lost in rediscovering oneself and transitioning into a healthier perspective of life, you are doing pretty well. It made me more tolerable, yet, taught me to never give up or compromise my idea of happiness for love.

Hopefully by now, you have learned to laugh with yourself. There are times when we will play the clown. Life is so much more enjoyable when we lighten up and forego perfection. Remember, "Nobody's Perfect." We can all be thankful for that.

CLARITY

We all must find our own way home. So, slow down. Usually, that thing which is totally unknown to us is what we are seeking to find.

Clarity means seeing it all… the good, the bad, the ugly… It leads to gaining perspective.

For so long, I was impedingly oblivious, as to what love truly is. Learning the boundaries around what it is not has helped me to discover what it is. Love is not suffering. Love is not expectation. It is a choice.

We all have a past. With purpose, my ex-husband wandered in and out of my life. The ones, who caused us the most pain, often offer the greatest lessons. Objective investigation will help us learn from the past.

When we accept our past, we can relieve ourselves from environmental and existential depression. Accepting our own past is a choice. Often times, accepting means moving on.

It was an unhealthy love. I had to let it go. He may have a beautiful heart, but it needed to be open to me for healthy love to grow between us. Someone who really loved me would want to help me grow and become my best self.

Besides, no matter how good of a woman I was, I could never be good enough for a man who was not ready. Remember, living is easier than dying and we just survived the death of our marriage. Do you realize how strong we are?

I did not know the weight of all I was carrying until I felt the freedom from its lifting. When it comes to love, there are so many different types of it. Learn by heart, in one form or another, we are loved.

There are many seasons of the heart. Keep it open even through the vulnerable and painful times. It is meant to bleed, abundantly. Love will come again and again.

We all have an unlimited capacity to love… if we choose to. The key is finding someone who loves you the way that you are. And that comes easily for some of us, especially those of us who consider ourselves aware and evolved.

Love is simple. Keep it simple.

RADIANT RELATIONSHIPS

Radiant Fairy Tales

by Shenetta Matthews

I have often wondered where the idea of fairytales and hopeless romantics came from, and if it is something attainable. As a little girl, I've watched countless stories on love, and dreamt of the day that my life would turn out that way.

I have spent many days playing games to predict my future, as if they were a compass to the path I should take. And as I grew up, I held on to the belief that the fairytale I imagined about my love life would eventually become a reality. After kissing a few frogs, my Prince did come, but not in the way I had fantasized about for all of those years.

My husband and I are from different states. College put us on common ground. We ran in some of the same circles, but never really got to know each other while enrolled in college. It was not until after we graduated, and met at the Single's Ministry at church, that we began to interact with each other.

During one of our break-out sessions, he told me he needed a job and I was able to connect him with a few leads. We did not talk much after that, but I ran into him from time to time. He finally landed a job with the company I worked for, and he needed some type of immunization before starting. I had already begun working there, but was not aware that I needed it as well.

Our appointments happened to be on the same day, but the times of appointment had me leaving as he was coming. Another friend of mine was there as well, because she needed the same proof of immunization.

After running into him, they began to inquire about each other, with me being the middle person. I was hoping to help them make a love connection, but the more I tried to connect them, the more he and I began to talk about life. This is where our friend ship began.

We started working for the same company, but in different locations. While at work one day, our front office secretary asked me about my personal life. We had had plenty of conversations about the future jobs, shopping, and other fun stuff, but we never really spoke about my personal life. On this particular day, she kept inquiring about my boyfriend.

I told her that I did not have one, and was not looking at the present time. She told me that she was on a mission to find my HUSBAND. I laughed it off, and went on about my daily duties.

About a month later, she had been reassigned to another building to be closer to home and have better working hours. I was a little sad that I would no longer share a laugh with her when I came into the office, but this type of transition normally happens when the opportunity presents itself.

One afternoon, a few weeks after she left, I received a phone call in my office. It was my office buddy. She gave me the updates on her family, her new position, and asked how things were for me. She sounded so excited on the phone.

After we had caught up on each other's lives, she told me that she had found my husband and that she wanted to introduce us. I laughed and told her that she was funny. She said, "Hold on, I want you to speak with him."

A deep voice said "Hello." At this point I am at a loss for words. I could not believe that she was serious and had placed some RANDOM guy on the phone with me! He said, "Hello" again, and this time the voice sounded familiar. I KNOW THIS VOICE! I said, "Hello." We both called each other's name, hesitantly.

Immediately there is an eruption of laughter. He informed me that my office buddy had been telling him about a young lady that she wanted to introduce to him as a potential mate.

We continued to laugh. He explained to her that he knows me already, and that we were good friends. He left the company shortly thereafter, but we kept in touch.

A year later, I needed a job, and he was able to help me get hired at his place of employment. Upon my arrival, people were so amazed at how well we worked together. Our work chemistry always caused people in the company to think we were dating or married. We always explained that we were JUST FRIENDS.

After working to make our department solid, we really began to learn more about each other. It was there that we became the best of friends. He got to know the real me, not my representative, as I did him. Even though he became my best friend, I still had no romantic interest in him. At this time, I was still waiting for MY prince to come.

After developing a strong friendship of about a year, when everyone thought we were either dating or married, we gave in to the "peer pressure" and decided to give dating a try. (This happened after I left the company of course.) Needless to say, it was meant to be! Three years of dating and we were getting engaged.

The wedding ceremony was beautiful, and all was well. I finally kissed my Prince, and thought we would live happily ever after. Six months later, and my husband was diagnosed with CANCER! Did I just say CANCER?! In my mind, I'm thinking how could

105 this be because my husband works out DAILY, eats right, and doesn't participate in at-risk behaviors. It was just six months ago that my fairytale came true, and now this nightmare. We were told that it was in stage IV, and that the prognosis could be good, if things go well with the treatments.

We were also told that we probably would not be able to have children, due to the chemotherapy treatments. I could not believe that this was happening to me, at this time. I was not sure of anything, anymore. The one thing that helped me keep my sanity was my husband's positivity.

He looked at it as a weight we had to lift to help strengthen our faith and our relationship. We treated his chemotherapy sessions as a date…bringing movies and popcorn or lunch. The others cancer warriors looked forward to us coming because we MADE a bad time, a good time!

Fast forward to now, and things have turned out really well. My husband's cancer scans were clear after the first three rounds of chemotherapy. He still had to complete all six rounds, but he has been cancer free for eight years.

We have TWO beautiful children; a boy and a girl. And even though we had to endure some setbacks, I do believe that we are on the journey to our happily ever after!

As I look back over things, I finally understand that fairytales do not mean that everything is always great.

Some of the most meaningful and radiant things come out of times of despair.

It was in the darkest of days that I felt the closest to my husband, and had the most love for him. During this time, we received random acts of kindness. When my husband left the company that employed him during his battle with cancer, he was paid for hundreds of sick hours that were donated.

People said that our love for each other, our families, and our community inspired them to show love to us. When a relationship is radiant, it emits light on people and places. I've learned that when you bring sunshine into lives of others, it's hard to keep it from your own.

RADIANT RELATIONSHIPS

Radiant Trust

by Tamala Davis

A radiant relationship can be a relationship with your mate, family, friends, or co-workers. Relationships need a foundation to grow on. As it says in The Bible, "Whatever a man sows, this he will also reap"- Galatians 6:7. The top three items you need to sow a Radiant Relationship is trust, communication, and commitment.

"A relationship without trust is like a car without gas, you can stay in it all you want, but it won't go anywhere." – Unknown

TRUST is key a relationship – Individuals need to feel secure, know that a person has your best interest at heart. Trust means I can lower my guard and show vulnerability with no hesitation or worry about being wounded. A few years ago, I went to Paris for work with several co-workers.

One day after work me, my friend Sara, and one of our vendor representatives who we'll call Dan decided to go to a night club. I knew Sara had a liking for Dan so at first I told her I didn't want to feel like the third wheel but she assured me this night was about going out to have fun on our last night in Paris, so I agreed to go.

We walked to a dance club that was a mile or so away. This night club was all that we imagined. A big two-story building, three huge colorful spotlights moving outside, it was full of people, and jam-packed with fun.

We grabbed drinks and danced with the crowd and even found our way into the VIP area. We were having a Grand time laughing and people watching.

I told Sara I was going to the bar to grab our next round, she nodded in acknowledgement. I wiggled my way over to the bar, grabbed the drinks, and literally had to sway with the crowd to return to the VIP section, but there was no Sara or Dan.

I sat for a few songs thinking they were on the dance floor but after 30 minutes I began to wonder where they were. I got up and looked around but all I could see was a swarm of people but none had the face of my girlfriend Sara or our rep Dan.

I decided to look around to find them, I moved with the crowd around the club a few times but no sight of them and now I'm starting to panic. I decided to look outside thinking they may have gone out for some fresh air.

Outside there was a crowd of people smoking in conversation, I noticed the line at the entrance was still down the block and around the corner but no sight of Sara or Dan.

I went to security to give them a description of my workmates but by the blank look on his face he didn't understand my Southern English American accent.

At this point I was flustered and worried. It was 3am, I had had a few drinks, and I was in a foreign country.

I didn't know if I was in Taken or Left Behind! I wasn't sure what to do, stay and call the police, should I start walking to the hotel in hopes of seeing them on my way, and do I even remember how to get back to the hotel?

So many questions…. Feeling alone, and vulnerable, my eyes started to tear up, then I heard the voice that comes when my nerves get the best of me "Head up, stay strong, fake a smile, move on." I wiped my eyes, prayed, and I started to walk to the hotel.

I did pretty well in remembering how to return to the hotel until I came to a fork in the road. I couldn't remember which way to go.

I looked down one street, it was empty, the other had two people lying on the sidewalk speaking French to each other and one yelled something to me.

That definitely was not the street I was going to go down so I walked down the one that was unoccupied. As I got to the end of the street I could see the top of our hotel. I feel it was God that placed those people on the other street so I'd know which way to go!

I finally made it back to the hotel and asked the front desk clerk to call Sara's room, she did and there was no answer. I left a note telling Sara I was in my room and to please call me when she arrived so I'd know she was safe. I went to my room looked at the clock it was 4:06am.

I lay across my bed and closed my eyes, when I opened them again it was 7:17am! I jumped up and called Sara's room again, no answer. At this point it's time to call the police. I went downstairs and ran into another colleague.

The fear must have been on my face; he asked me what was wrong. I told him I was looking for Sara and before I could get into the story he told me he had just left her and Dan at breakfast.

I was so relieved but just as I was settling in my happiness my heart started beating rapidly. I had been so worried and left a note for her to contact me and she was at breakfast?! Anger started to brew because I thought I had been unjust by leaving the club or not calling the police right away.

I went to the breakfast area and there she was shining like a brand new penny. I walked to the table and she said, "Good Morning Sunshine. Why do you look so rough?"

I knew I needed to answer this question without it ending with her wearing the, hollandaise sauce. I replied, "I've been worried about you, I couldn't find you and Dan at the club."

I explained my whole ordeal and asked if she received the message I left for her. She said, "Oh, I didn't make it back to my room last night" and gave me the sin grin. I knew at that point that I put my trust in someone who didn't have the same expectations in friendship.

I turned to her and said I would have never left you anywhere to fend for yourself especially in a different country. You have definitely shown me who you are and I will never put myself in this position again. Saddened, I turned and went back to my room. We haven't spoken about this incident since.

"When the trust account is high, communication is easy, instant, and effective."— Stephen R. Covey

Secondly, communication is an important key. Every relationship should have a goal. Stephen Covey says, "Begin with the end in mind." For example, you have a mate that you want to marry and spend your life living with in a townhouse with a cat.

Your mate wants to marry you but wants to live in a two story house with four kids and two dogs.

You may have established that you want to be married but there are two very different goals in mind for that marriage. It's essential that you go more in depth about each other's goals.

Discuss what the common "end" looks like (the goal), then verbally walk through the steps it will take to manifest the goal, and finally live it and communicate through any obstacles!

My sister and I grew up in two different cities our common parent is our dad. We grew up seeing each other on holidays and in the summer. We enjoyed our times together but rarely got to see each other during our birthdays because we were attending school.

We both love birthdays, because of this we agreed to be together for one of our birthdays every year.

We've taken great trips together and made some very fond memories to fill the past ones missed. My sister and I talked about the goal – having birthday memories, walked through the steps – taking a trip every year for one of our birthdays, and we live it - every year on an island, beach, or fun destination.

We understand that life happens and if one of us can't fulfill the goal, we communicate and make alternate plans. It's simple!

"Commitment means staying loyal to what you said you were going to do, long after the mood you said it in has left you." - Unknown

Last but certainly not least, commitment is a vital part of relationships. To commit is to carry out or perpetrate "to do" what you say you'll do. Sounds easy but people are disappointed by the lack of commitment every day.

We learn about commitment at a young age. When our parents tell us what they're going to do something it's a commitment.

I'll take you to the store for a treat if you're good at school tomorrow, this weekend we'll make pancakes for breakfast, this year for your birthday we're going to Disney World. It's their commitment to act on their words.

If your parents always followed through then you'll probably do the same as an adult. If they did not and this type of disappointment was a part of your childhood you probably give and accept this behavior.

This is important in all life relationships because it's linked to your character. When you commit you are giving yourself to that situation through the peaks and valleys until completion. Whether it is your education, being there for your best friend, or committing to be healthier this year, it's all the same.

There was a man who met a woman at a restaurant on July 13, they dated and then married. On the thirteenth of every month they would have lunch at this restaurant. This went on for much of 35 years. The woman became ill and passed on.

Their daughter asked her dad if she could take on this standing date with him, he happily agreed. A few years later the dad was diagnosed with Alzheimer's and eventually had to live at an assisted living facility.

He had his struggles with daily life but when his calendar showed the thirteenth of any month he would dress up and tell the nurse he was going to have lunch with his beloved wife.

The nurses thought it was sweet that he may not remember present day affairs but because of their love, in his mind he would never miss the commitment he gave his wife!

"What greater thing is there for two human souls, than to feel that they are joined for life-to strengthen each other in all labor, to rest on each other in all sorrow, to minister to each other in all pain, to be one with each other in silent unspeakable memories at the moment of the last parting?" - George Eliot, Adam Bede

RADIANT RELATIONSHIPS

Mirror Mirror on the Wall
by Amanda North

Most of us have at least one, if not several relationships in our lifetime. We have a multitude of ways we can experience these relationships. We can be in relationship with our friends, our work our family, ourselves, and yes – romantic relationship – with our partner or significant other.

The definition of "relationship" is:

noun

1. a connection, association, or involvement.
2. connection between persons by blood or marriage.
3. an emotional or other connection between people: the relationship between teachers and students.
4. a sexual involvement; affair.

according to *Dictionary.com*. By this, anything we are in connection with – we are also entering into a some form of relationship. The concept of connection means we are together and not separate. When we are in experience of relationship with another being, thing, or concept, we are fully connected and may have an experience of familiarity and being one.

This can be especially true when we connect with another human being. As we move through the relationship, the experience can draw out many emotions, processes or feelings about ourselves.

We may even feel triggered emotionally or otherwise. These moments can be our biggest teachers. These moments can be our mirror!

Here we will focus on relationships to the lovely human beings that show up in our lives. These relationships can ultimately provide us amazing insight into who we are and provide opportunities for us to grow as people and in relationships.

When we are born into our family, we have no control over who they are and what that may look or feel like to us. Most of us spend a lifetime learning how to love and relate to our families better. This is why family gatherings and holidays can be a mixed bag of feelings and emotions for some.

We spend our lives growing and learning who we are as individuals, which may or may not be in harmony with our family and the values which raised us.

Sometimes as we grow older, we find out things we never knew of some of our love ones when we were in childhood. We may begin to realize our family is full of people that have their own thoughts, loves, passions and struggles.

As we explore our family dynamic, we often are the most triggered emotionally by our siblings or parents. It feels they have a tendency to know right where to push our buttons. This interaction can create quite a stir for some.

But what if the button that is pushed is showing us something about ourselves in the process? What if we are learning more of ourselves and even possibly how to release and find a way to create more love?

Ah yes, I know it is easy to say – maybe even a novel concept – but in the moment can be quite challenging to do. However, what if the person we may be in conflict with is actually holding up a mirror for us to see where we can emotionally release, learn to soften and where growth in our self can occur?

From here, we get to choose our response – to blame, accuse, fight, or bring in more love for our self, the other, and the situation in the moment.

Often we choose to respond by blaming, accusing, finger-pointing or even name-calling. The last can be especially true for siblings, no matter what age. What if we allowed that situation to be a mirror seeing what or maybe where it is we are participating, and how to shift into something different? Maybe we can shift into love!

In romantic relationships the mirror can be even bigger. It has been said that when we are attracted to another, it is something in that person we love and see in ourselves. Wow!

What a gift to have a living, breathing mirror of ourselves to relate to and to see ourselves and all of our idiosyncrasies and all of our bliss. In the beginning, we are typically infatuated and bringing our best to the table.

We are reflecting all the loving, sweet, yummy parts of ourselves and reflecting them back into the relationship. Simultaneously, we see the same qualities in our new partner and are "in love" with them and who they are.

We are in love with what we see familiar and love in ourselves. A bond is created and we make a choice that we want to enter into this relationship with another.

We connect – we join. This now is different than the family dynamic where there was no choice. Here – in romantic relationship – we choose! And when we choose, we are happy, kind, loving, and see only the good in our new partner.

Then somehow, somewhere, at some point we inevitably run into conflict. There is a disagreement, and argument, or even fight.

What happened? Where did that person that was sweet, kind, and loving go? Where is the person with so much goodness that we chose to love? And here is where opportunity knocks. What is this person reflecting back to us that we may be dissatisfied within ourselves?

What if this person is just holding up a mirror for us to see what it is in us that we wish was different or may want to change? Where we can bring more love and compassion for ourselves, our partners and the situations that are allowing us to see? Yet, when it shows up we can tend to blame our partners.

Now, sure there are times that we can have conflict over miscommunication, we thought one was supposed to pick up the children at 5pm and the other 4pm and there was a lapse.

We can have simple disagreements in taste as in one person wants to go to one event and the other has a workshop in mind they would rather attend.

These are simple differences. But here, we are talking about personal disagreements when we start to feel attacked or thinking we may be with the wrong person, or at the very least, this is not the person we fell in love with.

So if we got into this relationship because we wanted connection, how do we maintain the connection of relationship even when we start to experience conflict?

Perhaps we can see the relationship as a gift of learning and growth – as a mirror reflecting back to us where we can see ourselves in a more objective light.

After all, we are all here on this planet to learn and grow in ways beyond physical and mental. We have emotional and spiritual work here as well.

Whatever that may look like to you – a relationship can offer a challenging mirror that allows that growth to happen. Lucky for us, it can be the most rewarding, sweet, yummy, lovely work we will ever do.

Sometimes these mirrors are not a direct match of apples to apples. As in, if we are upset with our partner for being disconnected, maybe we too are disconnected. Often this is the case, but other times we may just want more connection.

So instead of being upset with your partner, you see how you could offer to change the situation. Maybe you make more effort to connect, communicate, and be present. Staying aware of what may come up is key.

It has been said that the most spiritual work we can do is to get into relationships. We will grow leaps and bounds if we choose. Our eyes will be opened to parts of ourselves and vulnerabilities will arise. This is why many of us choose not to enter into relationships.

Some would rather blame others for things they see in themselves. We can jump from relationship to relationship when things get tough, or we may put walls up with our family, friends or co-workers instead of being open and vulnerable, allowing the process to open our hearts and our minds to what can be an opportunity for more love.

How can we allow our relationships to be used as a mirror and open us to a new understanding of the deepest part of ourselves? We can begin by listening to our hearts and staying in touch with ourselves.

We deepen our awareness of who we are, what we need, how we give, and what may be uncomfortable for us while in relationship.

We can stay vulnerable and aware as we enter into each experience, including conflict, and see it as a direct reflection of a part of ourselves.

As we begin to see and feel what arises in us, we can decide how to address the issue within ourselves or the situation to bring more love, compassion and awareness into the relationship.

When we do this, we can heighten our bliss, blossom more joy, and deepen relationship to ourselves and our mirror partner offering reflection for them. If we can work together in harmony – learning and growing – we can ultimately strengthen our relationships in the world.

Social Media Social

by Lindsey Rhodes

Relationships: the way in which two or more concepts, objects or people are connected or the state of being connected. Think about that for a second…are we not all connected somehow? The air we breathe…the energy we exude…the emotions we feel extended to all the we know?

Is it really about two or more? Or is it really about just one? Self? If there is truly no relationship with yourself, how would you even possibly engage in a relationship with someone, something, or somewhere else?

Culture today tells us we need to maintain and improve all the relationships that exist in our world. A romantic partner, our family, our professional relationships as well as our friends or acquaintances at best. Now more than ever, our friends transcend globally thanks to the social media mecca. The authenticity of relationships seems so far less genuine than they ideally appear.

In such a busy technologically driven society, all of our relationships are sustained through *Facebook, Instagram, Twitter, Match.com* etc. We are constantly texting and are engaged in false identities of relationships, myself included.

The filtered images, the texting conversations, updates we all shared through social media is a perceived notion of what we want others to see of us. We have all been allowed to create a beautiful kaleidoscope of an ever-changing world we only see through the "rainbowed" tunneled vision.

It is terrifying these days. The connection to our authentic selves is almost extinct. What do we do in order to serve ourselves? It is constantly driven into our psyche that we need to work harder, we don't make enough money, our house isn't nice enough, we don't have the perfect partner. Are all of these false expectations of our own insecurities?

We as a self-need to feed our souls full of self-love to banish all the self-criticism and pessimistic thoughts?

We constantly seek the validation through others, via social media for praise, body image, humor, sarcasm, and undoubtedly hurt and anger. How many times has someone...typically a "friend" of yours gone on a serious rant in order to get some sort of action or reaction from you?

We feel it our duty as a member of this social media society to respond without any hesitation from most people? We are driven on impulse and overreaction of the matter, before there is even a second thought of a deep breath, meditation, a moment of silence or practicing patience and kindness.

Ask yourself, how important is self-love? Would you feel whole without social media? How many of these people that are your friends co-exist in your daily life? Maybe, close to 15 to 20 people... scrolling through the news feeds, updates, pictures, tagging people?

Think about how much time we would save in our day? Really, add up all the time that we spend on our phones, computers, iPads, whatever. To expand upon all the creative aspects that we all are.

Ideas that we inhibit or dull down due to our obsessive need to check in compulsively with social media. Honestly, we even create pseudonyms for ourselves to make ourselves seem cool, or innovative for having a clever username.

What would we do with all of his amazing time that we never get back? We could start that book that has been sitting on our nightstand for months. What about that awesome pottery class that *Facebook* ironically keeps suggesting for you?

Something new and exciting like ballet lessons, getting an amazing massage or facial that we never feel like we can justify spending the money on, but we love so much.

All of these little things that we continually shy away from are hindering our self-love relationships. Conquering...doing something alone is not only gratifying, but completely liberating. You feel pristine and untouchable. Full of joy and exuberance!

This leads me to ponder the thought of living in the present moment with myself. The Universe knows no time. We create the boundaries around ourselves. Wanting to create the power of the here and now.

Social media cripples us with the constant reminder of the past whether it be positive or negative...Like the app *Timehop*, that is just another marketing tool to convince us that we NEED social media.

I never want to go back. I am constantly trying move forward, be love, manifest goodness in myself and others I choose to surround myself with. Choosing my relationship with myself supremely before anyone or anything else.

What time do we take to appreciate our mind, body, and soul? Holding yourself with a higher regard, controlling your thought processes. Only allowing in the good. Making the right choices for our authentic self.

Turning off the tv, silencing your phone, going to yoga, walking within nature, eating local food, taking a relaxing bath, enjoying your favorite music with a glass of wine.

The beauty of it is, all of these rituals are effortless and easy. We have to make the conscious decision to listen to our inherent voice of reason – our intuition. Putting these words on paper, speaking them into existence is much easier said than done.

Making time and space that is purposeful for ourselves feels selfish. Feeling as if we need to earn the right to have these quiet moments of self-love, and honor for our peace of mind and overall wellness.

This indeed is a restriction we put upon ourselves because we have been told one time or another that we are not worthy of these merits.

Truth be told, just opening our eyes and getting out of bed every day is a graceful deed. Let me be the one to proclaim these affirmations for you. YOU DESERVE IT ALL. YOU ARE LOVE!!!

Even if it is a short mantra for the day, say it out loud with conviction. Create an intention that holds you and your actions to yourself accountable. Maybe it includes something simple as smiling at a co-worker you are not especially fond of. Buying a stranger a cup of coffee. Refusing to criticize yourself and others.

Laughing – this is a hard one for some people that I find baffling. Laughing is one of the most healing emotions you can do for yourself. Even if it is something so petty and silly it releases negative and stressful tension. It's true, proven scientific fact!

Self-love is something that is obsolete for some. When you ask someone what is self-love, or a self-relationship that they have with themselves they have no idea. Optimism and hope are two words that don't resonate.

I have friends that I don't EVER talk to on the phone or face-to-face who live in the same city, but will comment on every post that I have ever made. These are the people I want to reach out to and try to understand why?

Choosing to emit self-love and knowing that I have a relationship with myself makes all my relationships easier.

Allowing myself time and space to connect with my spirit every morning is one of my most insightful times of the day. The quite essence of myself with a hot cup of coffee is part of my self-love ritual and it is extremely important to me.

Watching the sun creep in through the shades, candles burning to creating the soft illuminating light allows peace before a hectic day ahead.

Without this time every day, I would be evading myself of the magic and love I know that I possess. Protecting the sanctity of my morning coffee ritual is imperative for my sanity. I encourage all of you to do the same. Be the love and light that you know you are and deserve.

Human Connection

by Sara Smith

Human connection is such a vital part of our lives.

Most of us are surrounded by people the majority of our day whether it be at our places of employment, our homes with our families, restaurants, stores and even on social media such as *Facebook, Instagram, YouTube, Twitter,* etc.

There are times when we can even be on overload from all the connection we have to others and need that solitude to replenish our souls. For reflection…To refuel so that we can go back out in this big world to connect again and to inspire or be inspired, to create and to conquer.

You can be the most beautiful person in the world or the wealthiest person in the world, but none of that will mean a thing if you are all alone and do not share any genuine human connection.

We need this connection to share emotions, to create, to learn and to make not only the world a better place but to make us as individuals better.

Being open is important in making a connection as you just never know when or where this may happen – but also more importantly with whom. It can happen when you least expect it and with people of all sizes, shapes, ages and color.

I have had some really genuine connections that almost felt magical and as if the Universe made this person just for me to share my ideas and thoughts with and they with me.

It might happen in a crowded elevator, in a public restroom, waiting in line at the bank, etc. but when that connection happens, what an overwhelmingly incredible feeling and genuine connection it is!

But has there ever been a time when you met someone that you felt no connection with whatsoever? Nothing. Nada. Zilch. Not meaning whether you liked them, loved them or even really disliked...but just that you felt not one inkling of connection.

The only thing you felt was indifference. Such an odd and unsettling emotion since we as human beings rely on connection to communicate and to evolve. We need to feel some type of emotion - good or bad. But we crave and need to feel something.

Thankfully this has been a one-time occurrence for me. But quite unfortunately, it was about someone that was detrimental in my family dynamics. My stepson - my husband's son!

When my stepson first came into my life, he was a mere four years old. Just a child. Most children at that age are cute and cuddly, fun and playful, curious and inquisitive.

All qualities I admire and love. But my stepson was none of those things. He was difficult and unhappy, demanding and very needy. Even though he was a child, I had ZERO connection to him. Was something wrong with me?! Believe me - I asked myself this over and over.

I am a mother and have two biological children and would consider myself to be a very nurturing mother who not only loves her children but prayed to have children just like them.

I have always been drawn to children and them to me. Coming from a large Catholic family, there were always children around whether it was brothers and sisters, cousins, church gatherings, etc.

I adore my family and friends and truly love to be around people. How can I feel this disconnection to someone who is so young and will be part of my life for years to come? Was the success of my new family doomed?

Would it be all my fault if this relationship didn't work out due to my lack of connection to my stepson?

What was I doing wrong? What was I lacking as a stepparent? Was I just a horrible person because I felt this way? And not only did I feel this way about another human being but my own stepson.

Oh my, there must be a special place in hell for me is what would go through my mind. I spent many nights meditating, writing, praying and, yes, even researching into who I could talk to or what I could do to change this feeling.

Researching only made me feel even more isolated. Isolation was the opposite of what I wanted to feel as I wanted connection. Was the Universe not understanding that I wanted CONNECTION?!

Have you ever tried anything and everything but only thing that grew was your frustration?

Yes, that was me. For years I tried a variety of things but nothing I did helped and, if anything, I only grew more frustrated with myself and him because that void only grew wider and wider until it really felt hopeless.

But I diligently continued to search within myself and elsewhere to find answers or even any insight as to what I could change or do differently.

Did I not connect with him because of his mother? Did I resent him for the time he took my husband away from me as well as the rest of the children? Did I just not like myself and the role of being a stepmother? So many questions and not one answer in sight.

I tried to spend time alone with him or with some of his siblings doing fun things, took him places that he would show interest in going to, took him to places that I loved so that he could get to see and experience new things, but none of this helped and it only brought out all the qualities I found undesirable in a person. In both him and me!

Even my own biological children felt the same way I did so it only made a very difficult situation of blending families together even more difficult. My children complained about him which only added fuel to my fire of this "difficult" child. What was I going to do?

Never before in my life have I been faced with this and I needed it to be resolved in my heart for some peace. I grew to dread his visits and for a long time, I would find excuses to not be around when it was time for him to visit. Any excuse was a good excuse for my absence during his visits.

Avoiding the situation only made it worse. And you know the saying, "what you resist only persists"? Yes, this was like a dark cloud that followed me wherever I went.

So not only was it a hard situation between my stepson and me, but between my sons and their stepbrother, between my husband and my sons, and between me and my husband.

Even my husband would be frustrated with his son for being so difficult and then my husband and I would argue about it all. What an evil viscous cycle and would it ever end? What a miserable situation and I couldn't find a resolution fast enough.

I looked for the good in him as surely we all have at least one good, redeeming quality. Can you believe I even struggled finding that one quality?

After years of this inner turmoil, I finally noticed he would read a children's book every once in a while. Now a love for reading is something I truly know about and so I would buy books I thought he would like. I would read to him, take him to bookstores, the library, etc.

Hallelujah! Bingo! We had a winner! So for years that is all I talked to him about. And I mean that was the only topic of our conversation. It became our common denominator but we only needed one to have a connection.

When he started reading books, he found so many other things that interested him and his whole world opened up/ He discovered more about himself. Not only did he find out more about himself, but I found that I could work through a very difficult situation.

Did it happen overnight? Did it happen after just a few tries? Absolutely not. It took mindful dedication along with a deep desire to change my outlook along with his.

Patience is a virtue, but it definitely is not one I possess so I swear when I tell you this was a very hard process for me. The reading and sharing of books turned into his love of eating. I love to cook, so now we had another commonality and connection.

Do we have in-depth and deep conversations about religion or politics or an endless list of other subjects? No, but we don't need to. Our connection was finally made after trial and error and lots of persistence.

I am very proud to say that my stepson is now a college graduate and a young adult with a real job. It has become a real joy to watch this young man who has worked through difficult situations and turmoil in his life now being a loving, giving and productive human being.

I am also proud to call him my "bonus child" and instead of anticipating his visits with dread, I look forward to them.

Can you believe that? The connection I thought I would never have! I know as I look back at it all, I find it hard to believe. We have to keep searching for answers. Giving up or giving in is unacceptable.

Time and patience, prayer and persistence will get you through anything. Human connection is that important. Sometimes it doesn't come easily but when you finally make that connection, it is such a magical and vital part to our becoming a better human being.

And isn't that what life is about anyway, making those connections so that we are all better and loving individuals so that we can make this world a better place for everyone?

How Can I Make My Relationships Not Suck?
by Mai White

The self-help industry is acutely aware that you want it right now, whatever it is. They are clear that you want an enviable life that includes dynamic and fulfilling relationships, and that you want that now.

That is why books such as Mira Kirshenbaum's *The Gift of a Year, How to Achieve the Most Meaningful, Satisfying and Pleasurable Year of your Life*, sell.

I am not sure what I am supposed to do after that year, but I am sure that there is another book out there that is happy to give me the next plan of action that I need to execute. But, this brings up a question for me.

What if I cannot afford a year to spend the time, money and energy that it might take to get what I want out of my life, as the book prescribes? Indeed, I might want some solution that is faster, less expensive and not as emotionally taxing.

So, I might hurry to my local library and get Michele Weiner-Davis' book, *Change Your Life and Everyone In It*.

The title is a little unnerving but I want to read it because it claims it will help me to Transform Difficult Relationships, Overcome Anxiety and Depression, Break Free from Self-Defeating Ways of Thinking, Feeling, and Acting in One Month or Less.

Wow! Really??? While I am perusing the other self-help books, I could pick up Kevin Leman's book, *Have a New Kid by Friday*. "Awesome!" I exclaim, "Having a new kid is the number one thing I had on my 'to do' list for this week!"

I am overjoyed that my relationship with my child will suddenly become a seamless stream of beautiful conversations where obedience, peace and empathetic listening abound.

Although, I live in what has been coined as the "microwave society" so I might not want to wait until

Friday. So I might want to employ John Maxwell's wisdom that instructs me in his book that *Today Matters, 12 Daily Practices to Guarantee Tomorrow's Success.*

Make no mistake, those last three words were premeditatedly selected to motivate me, book in my left hand and my credit card in my right, to march to the nearest cash register.

As a person who values vulnerability and authenticity, I do not resonate with these titles that the author's selected. In fact, I think that the titles sound like something a used car salesman might say.

Nevertheless, I genuinely have no doubt that there is wonderful, useful information in all the literature that I just cited. I am sure that these authors are seeking to address some of our primal needs which is why those books are on the bestsellers list.

Indeed, it might be safe to say that we all pine for some sort of success, to triumph over all the adversity that life can bring, especially in our relationships.

I also think that it is human nature to want some sort of a guarantee, something that brings us security that includes a lifetime warranty.

I certainly wish that having deep, meaningful and fun relationships was as easy as ordering your groceries online where everything is guaranteed to be exactly as you have ordered it.

However, I have lived life for a while now and I have found that there are no guarantees in life (save death and taxes) and that quick and easy programs are not usually effective. Consequently, I feel more kindred with the title of my chapter, "How Can I Make My Relationships Not Suck?"

Why would I choose a title like that? My intent is not to be crass or negative. I just like "keepin' it real" and I do not buy into the propaganda of quick fixes in relationships. Truly, what I am offering in this chapter is certainly not written from some pious place but from my own vat of challenging experiences.

The reality is life can be excruciatingly painful at times and no one is exempt from the throbbing agony that can come from broken relationships.

Whether the source is from growing up in an alcoholic home, divorce, untimely death of a love one or being teased by fellow students at school, we all have experienced relational loss.

Sometimes people grieve openly and sometimes people bury their grief deep inside their souls. Sometimes the pain took place yesterday and sometimes the loss happened decades ago, but humans grow weary of the pain and more times than not, the hurt may not fade quickly.

This truth about relationships is what propelled me to choose my unconventional title.

The reason why books on relationships sell so well is that our need to connect with others is universal. There is actually a plethora of scientific research that can substantiate the claim that we are neurologically designed for connection.

Dr. Brené Brown, a well-known shame researcher, says, "We are wired for connection. It's in our biology.

As infants, our need for connection is about survival. As we grow older, connection means thriving- emotionally, physically, spiritually and intellectually.

Connection is critical because we all have the basic need to feel accepted and to believe that we belong and are valued for who we are." We all want to feel worthy and affirmed.

Feeling disconnected, on the other hand, tends to make people feel diminished, rejected, unworthy and unloved. Dr. Brown also says, "Experiencing those feelings often leads to a prevailing feeling of shame.

While dealing with feelings of isolation and shame can be part of the natural progression that happens in a relationship, disconnection becomes troublesome when it progresses into feelings of isolation.

By this I don't mean just a feeling of being alone or being lonely." Jean Baker Miller and Irene Striver, Relational-Cultural theorists from the Stone Center at Wellesley College, have strikingly captured the demoralizing nature of isolation.

They say, "We believe that the most terrifying and destructive feeling that a person can experience is psychological isolation. This is not the same as being alone.

It is a feeling that one is locked out of the possibility of human connection and of being powerless to change the situation.

In the extreme, psychological isolation can lead to a sense of hopelessness and desperation. People will do almost anything to escape this combination of condemned isolation and powerlessness."

If feeling connected in our relationships is so vital to our well-being, it begs the question, "How do we connect?"

I believe it begins by communicating. When I use the term communicating, I am referring to verbal and nonverbal communication as well as active listening.

To be clear, verbal communication provides the raw, informative and neutral data. Nonverbal communication is used to add the "flavor" – to show attitude and emotion to the otherwise "dry" data.

Active listening requires that the listener fully concentrates, understands, responds to and then remembers what is being said. All three communication components work in tandem for effective communication.

So if we talk to each other, we will feel connected?

Not necessarily. I am afraid that communicating effectively can be very challenging. The problem is what John L. Wallen calls, "The Interpersonal Gap."

Wallen defines the interpersonal gap as, "the degree of congruence between one person's intentions and the effect produced in the other.

If the effect is what was intended, the gap has been bridged. If the effect is the opposite of what is intended, the gap has become greater."

Wallen states, "You cannot have your own way all the time. Your best intentions will sometimes end in disaster, while at other times, you will receive credit for desirable outcomes you didn't intend. In short, what you accomplish is not always what you hoped."

It could be argued that the basic and recurring communication problem in relationships is the disparity between what you intend to communicate and the effect of your actions on others. In an attempt to make sense of the mystery in interpersonal communications, I will use Wallen's terms: "intentions," "effect" and "actions."

"Intentions mean the wishes, wants, hopes, desires, and fears that give rise to your actions. Intentions are private and are known directly only to the one who experiences them. For instance, I know my own intentions, but you must infer mine."

Wallen further says, "Effect refers to a person's inner response to the actions of another. We may describe the other's effect by openly stating what feelings are aroused by his actions. However, we are often unaware of our feelings as feelings.

When this happens, our feelings influence how we see the other and we label him or his actions in a way that expresses our feelings even though we are unaware of them."

In contrast to interpersonal "intentions" and "effects" which are private, "actions" are public and observable. They may be verbal ("Good Evening") or nonverbal (looking away as you pass someone on the street), brief (a pat on the hand), or extended (taking your child to the park).

Interpersonal actions are communicative. They include attempts by the sender to convey a message, whether or not it is received, as well as actions that the receiver responds to as messages, whether or not the sender intended them that way. (Wallen).

The speaker is trying to communicate his intentions or message. That individual is "encoding" which is the language, tone of voice and movement that he uses when speaking.

This is public. He is filtering how he communicates by his beliefs, judgements and past experiences which is how he perceives things.

Factors like age, culture, and religion play a part in this and it is the only "filter" that a person has to interpret what is going on around him. Everyone has a personal filter and no two filters are exactly alike.

Again, the action can be verbal, nonverbal or both. Then the listener, or the "receiver" will filter the action through his own personal filter, which will never be the exact same filter as the speakers.

When the speaker's intention misses the mark, the interpersonal gap occurs.

What I like to teach is HOW to bridge that gap. One of the main models I use in my work is called "The Awareness Wheel" designed by Millier, Wackman, Nunnally and Saline.

The purpose of The Awareness Wheel is to increase your awareness of what is going on in any given situation. With increased awareness, you can decide what your choices are. Lastly, you can communicate clearly and concisely to the other person or people, what you are experiencing.

The basic premise of The Awareness Wheel is that we are constantly having thoughts and feelings but we are more aware of some than others.

We are often more conscious of one area more than another area. For example, you may be more in touch with your feelings than your thoughts.

The authors explain that The Awareness Wheel map includes five zones to enable a person to more effectively process important information about themselves.

All five are present in your experience even though you may not be conscious of them. They become available when you tune into them and use them.

Sensing involves receiving data from your immediate external, physical world through the five senses: sight, sound, smell, taste and touch. ("I hear your voice becoming louder.")

Thinking involves assigning meaning to the sense data by filtering it through your internal world of memories, associations, insights, knowing's, dreams and hunches.

Thoughts are the meaning you make to help you understand yourself, other people and situations. ("I think you are scared.")

Feelings are your spontaneous responses to the match between your sensory data and your thought or wants in a situation. ("I'm happy.")

Wanting involves what you desire from a situation for yourself and others. ("I want to win this argument.")

Doing involves doing something based on sense date received, meaning assigned, feelings, and intentions. (I ask, "Are you upset?")

(Miller, Wackman, Nunnally and Saline)

After an event or issue transpires, you can "walk the wheel." Although you can jump into the wheel in any order, I find that it is most helpful to begin with what you are sensing. (I am noticing that your face is turning red). Then move to the thoughts, ("I think you are angry." or "I think you misunderstood me.)

Talk about what you are feeling, ("I feel irritated" or "I can hardly breathe I feel so scared.") Communicate what it is that you want, ("I want to end this conversation" or "I want to put this conversation on hold until we both calm down.")

By verbally or physically carrying out your "want," you are executing the "doing". Keep in mind that your output (what you say or do) is your listeners input, what they sense.

This model is just one example of how to increase your effectiveness in your communication and is really meant to heighten your awareness when you are trying to communicate something of importance.

It may feel artificial when you begin using the model but with some practice, you will be able to communicate with increased efficiency and accuracy.

In closing, I have discussed how the market is saturated with self-help books that surely have great information but can sometimes minimalize the pain we experience with their grandiose titles.

I have pointed out that we have a primal need for connection that can occur when good communication happens between people.

"The Interpersonal Gap" shows us why communication can often be difficult and the "Awareness Wheel" gives us a tool to help us with our "gap problem."

Relationships can suck and there is no magic pixie dust to make them perfect. It has not been my intent to focus on the destruction that relationships may have brought in the past but to offer some understanding of why relationships can be so challenging and to offer a tool that might aid in bringing some hope and healing.

Whether it be your partner, boss, friend or child, good communications skills are essential in connecting with others. I hope that you have enjoyed this little snippet on relationships.

It is my hope that what I have said resonates with you and that imbedded in my words are healing kernels of truth that have been expressed in candor. My "want" is that it helps you in your relationships so that you can experience more authentic, loving and radiant connections.

RADIANT RELATIONSHIPS

Dee, Momma is Dead
by Adia Moreno

March 17, 2011. I believe that day fell on a Thursday that year. It was the day after my 30th birthday. We had just recently purchased our first home and relocated from Alaska.

In addition, our youngest child had his very first birthday a few days prior and our oldest child turned 15.

This week I refer to as "Moreno Birthday Week" or the week of the third-decan Pisces. Three of our six family members' birthdays all fall on this week and now there was death amongst it. Most definitely a pivotal year that changed my complete existence.

"Dee, Momma is Dead." Those were the words my baby sister uttered to me that day. I can recall the day as if it was yesterday. The feelings that ravaged my body.

Although I was consumed with emotion, my soul was paralyzed, numb and 161 lifeless. As if my entire mind, body and spirit had fallen into a deep coma like trance.

My mother, Celia, who was diagnosed six months previously with stage-four breast cancer that had metastasized throughout her entire 47-year old body, was dead and I wasn't there for her.

There I was, barely 30 years old, mother of four, wife of active duty soldier, seasoned nurse who was absolutely clueless in regards to my identity and spirituality.

I felt I believed in God but my relationship with him was weak. I wasn't aware of his true existence because his presence wasn't objective.

I believed the rationale for my believed success in life was because of "me" and not due to the strength he provided to me. Even though I felt very accomplished in my endeavors in life, it was time that I recognized where the strength showered from.

Those moments were the turning point in my life where God made his presence known and made me sit down and acknowledge his presence.

In life, I've always had the ability to "bounce back" as I call it from stress and overcome obstacles. I always had my back up plan b, c and d just in case my initial plan was unsuccessful.

That was the way I navigated through life. Unfortunately, I didn't have a backup plan for my mother passing and what was to come.

Over the next couple of months, I found myself sleeping less and less through the night, waking every morning around 3am. Not exactly knowing why, I would find myself going to our oldest daughter's room and asking her questions…if she was okay and if anyone had ever done anything to her.

She would always respond, "No Mom. Why are you asking?" To this day, I have no idea what prompted me. I just did it intuitively.

I continued this for weeks until May 19, 2011. That was the moment that her response changed. Not only her response but our lives. She responded, "Yes, Mom. Your brother. He started having sex with me when I was six years old."

The trance-like state that had been over me for the last couple of months seemed to sweep away. I was awake. Wide awake.

After acknowledging her response and never once doubting her words, I returned to the master bedroom where my husband lay in a tranquil sleep. I nudged him and informed him what had occurred. He asked if she was telling the truth.

I couldn't believe I had just heard those words come out of his mouth. How dare he question it! There was never any doubt in my mind. It was almost as if he asked if the sun would rise in the morning. I responded, "Yes, and NEVER allow our child to know that you ever questioned her word."

Moments later, I reported the accusation and begin the process to have my brother prosecuted. Weeks went by and I continued sleeping less and less but my responsibilities kept increasing.

I was working full-time, I had the majority of the responsibilities managing the house due to my husband's Drill Sergeant assignment, and I continued the process of having my brother prosecuted.

At this time, I would find myself pacing the floor in the early hours of the morning again in the normal trance-like numb state.

During this time, my menstrual cycle became ever so ravage especially with my emotional mood swings that I had considered oral birth control but couldn't because I was still nursing our son. So, just going through the motions, I continued without any inclination of how my life would change so dramatically in the next few weeks.

Then it came in the mail. The report. The detailed report of the years of abuse that my daughter was subjected to that I was so blind to.

Even though I knew better, I sat down in the formal dining room and I read every word, sentence, paragraph and page after page.

My brother even attempted to abuse our youngest daughter when she was only two years old but our older daughter intervened. My soul was engulfed with so much anger, rage and guilt.

How could he countlessly and continuously time after time take my child's innocence and betray my trust? This wasn't a neighbor or friend I left my children with. This was my brother. My brother.

After reading the report, I sat there. I'm unaware of how long I sat in stillness. I just remember that was when I stopped sleeping.

About nine days passed without sleep. I continued through my days finding myself experiencing uncontrollable outbursts of tears, distress and anguish.

My husband was rarely home to sleep but was so exhausted that he wasn't aware of my mental state until he came home early one day and found me in a huddled fetal position the corner in our bedroom.

After talking with me, he knew that my sanity was questionable and unstable. So he took me to the ER where I voluntarily admitted myself to the inpatient psychiatric unit.

Upon admission, my agitation increasingly grew. I was transported by an officer to an inpatient unit away from the hospital. The building had was old and very much dated. The smells of bad body odor and mothballs were so unpleasant.

It was dark and devastatingly depressing. I had no idea where this place was and had tremendous anxiety in regards to my husband being able to locate me. He wasn't allowed to accompany me so I was alone.

So many thoughts raced through my mind. I've never felt so helpless and alone in my entire life. One of my greatest concerns was abandonment. What would I do if he never returned for me?

After being interviewed by one of the staff psychiatrists, I was deemed committable for observation. Luckily, I would not be staying at the asylum I was brought to that evening.

To my surprise, there was a new psychiatric wing for women that had just opened at the hospital two days prior. I was transferred by a police officer to the new unit.

Once brought to the unit, I was escorted behind lock doors to a room with staff. They proceeded to ask me question after question. It was never ending and all I could think about was my husband and children. I just wanted to go home.

My agitation grew and grew. That's when the proceeded to give me pill after pill and refused to tell me what they were. They simply said if I didn't take them, I wouldn't be allowed to go home.

I knew as a trained and licensed nurse that they were violating my rights, but I didn't care. I just wanted to go home. So I did what they told me to do. Hours went by and nothing. I was wide awake and pissed off. How dare they? Didn't they know who I was?

That's when the grandiose delusions began. I can't recall much after that. My next memory was being abruptly awaken by staff the next morning from a what I believed was my death.

Pissed beyond belief, I began to become quite irate with the staff. It had been over a week since I slept and months for any continuously sleep.

I was so exhausted. But none of that mattered. I knew I needed to talk to someone. Pastor, clergyman, chaplain and ASAP!

The first chaplain that was brought in was a judgmental asshole. I could see it all over him. I didn't even need to talk so I told him to get out. Later that day, I approached the nursing assistant that helped with my intake.

There was something about her that I could feel. She had the most empathy for me. I knew that if I asked her that she would bring the right person to me and she did just that.

I can remember him to this day. He was a small-framed, bald, fair-skinned, military chaplain with a very gentle discernment. I told him my story and the dream that I had where I died over and over again. I knew I had. There was no other explanation.

When I finally finished, with tears streaming from my face in hope that he would provide me with clarity, I waited for his response. When I looked up at him, I noticed that he was crying with me. It seemed as if an eternity had passed before he spoke. His response was....

"You didn't die. You were reborn."

ABOUT THE AUTHORS

More information on these
Holistic Coach co-authors
is available at
RadiantCoaches.com

Made in the USA
Columbia, SC
21 September 2022